# The **USES** of
# DIGITAL
# LITERACY

# The USES of DIGITAL LITERACY

## JOHN HARTLEY

Transaction Publishers
New Brunswick (U.S.A.) and London (U.K.)

First Transaction publication 2011
Copyright © 2009 by John Hartley.

This book is printed on acid-free paper that meets the American National
Standard for Permanence of Paper for Printed Library Materials.

Library of Congress Catalog Number: 2010012583
ISBN: 978-1-4128-1429-4
Printed in the United States of America

Library of Congress Cataloging-in-Publication Data
Hartley, John, 1948-
  The uses of digital literacy / John Hartley.
    p. cm. -- (Creative economy and innovation culture series)
  Originally published: St Lucia, Qld. : University of Queensland Press,
    2009.
  Includes bibliographical references and index.
  ISBN 978-1-4128-1429-4
  1. Mass media. 2. Digital media. 3. Literacy. 4. Digital communica-
tions. 5. Communication and technology. 6. Multimedia communications.
  I. Title.

P91.27.H37 2010
302.231--dc22

                                                    2010012583

**Dedicated, with his kind permission,
to Richard Hoggart**
- the 'mild-mannered Clark Kent of cultural studies'
(Hartley 2003: 25)

# Contents

*'The time to work for a commonweaith of civilizations is now.'*
Giovanni Arrighi, Iftikhar Ahmad & Min-wen Shih (1996)

# 1

# Repurposing Literacy
## 'There Are Other Ways of Being in the Truth'

## Dr Who?

Cultural and media studies in the Anglo-Australian tradition was founded more than fifty years ago by Richard Hoggart, whose book *The Uses of Literacy* (1957) set the agenda for educational and disciplinary reform in schools and universities, and whose trenchant views on what he saw as the *abuse* of literacy (Owen 2005), especially in entertainment media, found widespread public support. Hoggart focused on print media - the press, magazines, advertising and pulp fiction. Since then broadcast television has come and, although not gone, has begun to yield ground to successor media in the shape of online and mobile services. It is time for a reappraisal. What are the 'uses of literacy' in the era of multimedia?

Hoggart's importance lies not so much in the examples he chose, and certainly not in his judgements of individual items, but in his attempt to connect the inner life of the individual imagination with the growth of mediated meanings in democratising and commercial societies. His interest in literacy was in what ordinary people did with it as part of everyday culture, rather than as an instrumental skill for business, civic or religious purposes. Hoggart valued the bottom-up 'decent' values of working-class community over the 'candy-floss' world of commercial entertainment, but in the end he knew that the problem was not going to be solved by preferring one over the other. He spent a long career arguing for 'critical' literacy as a form of popular engagement with popular media. In this endeavour he did not presume that the tastes of intellectuals are best for everyone else. As he put it in an apt turn of phrase: 'there are other ways of being in the truth' (Hoggart 1957: 261).

Hoggart's own most famous public intervention into the popular 'uses of literacy' was to defend a commercial publisher from charges of obscenity. As a literary critic he was called as an 'expert witness'; his judgement that D.H. Lawrence's novel was not obscene but in fact 'puritanical' - because the characters in it were indeed pursuing their own way of being in the truth - helped to win the case (Paul Hoggart 2006). Naturally that led to extra readers for both *Lady Chatterley's Lover* (Lawrence 1960) and *The Uses of Literacy,* and to extra income for Penguin, which published both books. Indirectly it led also to the Birmingham Centre for Contemporary Cultural Studies, in the form of a cheque given to Hoggart by Sir Allen Lane, owner of Penguin Books, that enabled him to set it up (Hartley 2003: 20-7). The trial was later made into a TV drama, *The Chatterley Affair* (produced by BBC Wales in 2006), where the role of Richard Hoggart was played by David Tennant, better known as the tenth Dr Who.

**David Tennant as star witness Richard Hoggart in** *The Chatterley Affair*

According to Hoggart's elder son, Simon, the *Guardian* political columnist, Tennant got it just about right, albeit with one telling error:

> Dad is played by the wonderful David Tennant *(Blackpool, Casanova)* who has carefully prepared his appearance by watching old interviews, even studying newspaper pictures of the time and having a picture of Dad on his mobile phone. He's extremely convincing - the suit, the hair, the Yorkshire accent, and trickiest of all, the speech rhythms. The only thing wrong is his sideburns. To do this film he had to take 24 hours off from making *Doctor Who* in Cardiff and, as he explained, the sideburns wouldn't grow back in a day.
>
> There, I thought, was a kind of fame - to have researchers and costume directors pore over every detail of your appearance, then be seen in the witness box wearing Doctor Who's face furniture (Simon Hoggart 2006).

Reviewing the show, the TV critic for *The Times* - Hoggart's younger son, Paul - concurred:

'Was that OK?' asked David Tennant slightly nervously after he had done his turn as my father in court. It was great,' I said. 'You did really well.' And I meant it - about both of them (Paul Hoggart 2006).

Paul Hoggart commented: 'Perhaps the strangest effect of [Andrew] Davies's re-creation is that, despite everything, so many of the issues raised by the trial remain alive and unresolved today.' It is some of those issues that this book attempts to work through and eventually beyond.

## Making Discriminations

Richard Hoggart understood that in commercial democracies people can choose what media entertainments they like. Therefore, anyone motivated by a desire to promote 'critical' literacy and intellectual emancipation for all had better come to terms with what they do like, taking seriously the means people use to express themselves as well as the media they like and trust to tell them things, whether through pleasurable entertainment or painful home truths. This insight flew in the face of established intellectual authority. Since John Ruskin, Walter Pater and Oscar Wilde (in Art) and then through A.C. Bradley, I.A. Richards and F.R. Leavis (in Literature), and in a weird parody of industrial or scientific expertise, critics before Hoggart had felt entitled to claim exclusive expertise in the matter of judgement, evaluation and taste-formation, a claim that entailed a refusal of the same to lay populations and especially to people of 'lower' class (Carey 1992). The very purpose of the critic was to name the difference between the 'sublime' (art) and the 'cor blimey' (popular sensation) and to tutor the ignorant public in matters of 'discrimination', which was treated as the humanities equivalent of scientific specialised methodology.

Popularised among the educated classes by F.R. and Q.D. Leavis and their journal *Scrutiny*, that attitude persisted as a commonsense policy setting at least until Thatcherism. Perhaps the last time British literary critics were valued by people other than themselves was in the Annan Report on the *Future of Broadcasting* (1977); it was this report that eventually led to the establishment of Channel Four in 1982. The Annan Report offered literary critics as the representatives of critical citizenship, the antidote to medical experts and social investigators, especially in TV shows about sex:

> Their opinions need to be scrutinized by such people as literary critics or by shrewd men and women of the world; people who are accustomed to making discriminations about questions of value and right and wrong and who, not being overawed by the experts, would be skilled enough to put them under disconcerting cross-examination, and be quick to puncture pseudo-science masquerading as incontrovertible proof.

Hoggart himself was just the sort of critical citizen imagined here, and he maintained his own preference for 'hard-working, fair-minded intelligent laymen and women' over experts or partisans (Hoggart 1997: 289). A problem here, however, was that literary critics were not in fact 'laymen and women', but experts in their own narrow specialism - that of 'making discriminations'. The idea that such people could speak for the population at large when questions of 'sexual behaviour' arose in public discussion seemed risible even at the time (I was among those who mocked: see Goulden & Hartley 1982). It could also be seen as 'discriminatory' in a negative way, seeming to line critics up with established values and with forms of discrimination based on evaluating differences not just among texts but also among people, for instance by gender, race and class.

Hoggart had known the game was up twenty years earlier. The taste of the population could not be corralled into a universalist consensus on the say-so of *soi-disant* and self-selected intellectuals. It had become evident that their judgements were bounded by their own familial, age-group, class, gender, race, national and colonial status. Values - cultural as well as political and moral - were formed within the context of cultural specificity among increasingly differentiated demographics. Hoggart understood that those formed by 'other' experiences - other ways of being in the truth - were not *anti*-intellectual but came to wisdom by other means. Thus it became important to investigate the opportunities and temptations that non-intellectual citizens may encounter along that route, which led directly to the study of mediated entertainment in popular culture: in short to *The Uses of Literacy*.

Hoggart had a lot invested in the proposition that popular culture was a positive source of values and judgements (in the first half of *Uses*), even as he found fault with much of the entertainment fare destined for popular consumption (in the second half of *Uses*). But this remained a minority position, even on the Left, which continued to hold to a modernist and/or Marxist view that saw popular culture in opposition to intellectual culture, not to be trusted because it was prey to manipulation by powerful forces, from commerce to fascism, although oddly enough few literary intellectuals worried about popular culture being manipulated by *communism* - an exception being Anthony Burgess's 1962 novel *A Clockwork Orange,* where the youthful thugs' argot (called Nadsat) was infiltrated by Russian words (Nadsat being the Russian for the suffix -teen).

Suspicion of the popular remains an important strand of thought among intellectuals. Literary theorist John Frow, for instance, wrote in *Cultural Studies and Cultural Value:*

> There are clear limits to the extent to which it is possible for intellectuals to associate themselves with anti-intellectualism; and there are limits to how far they can or should suspend their critique of, for example, racism, sexism, and militarism (1995: 158).

Commenting on this passage, the critic Alan Sinfield observed that Frow intended to:

> reassess the wish, perhaps sentimental, of the middle-class intellectual to engage with popular culture: in practice, she or he will encounter there attitudes that are hard to take. Of course, one would not want to slide into an assumption that popular culture is fascist whereas high culture is enlightened (1997: xxv).

In Sinfield's formulation, intellectuals are by definition middle-class. Equally, popular culture is cast as non-middle-class, taking the 'popular' in popular culture to mean demotic (low) rather than democratic (wide), as if intellectuals are external to and therefore exempt from it. This manoeuvre is required in order to produce an opposition between intellectual and popular culture, so as to cast the latter as a 'site of struggle' wherein progressive forces might contest those apparently fascistic tendencies among the 'masses'.

This is indeed the Althusserian program for cultural studies that was elaborated by Hoggart's successor Stuart Hall (1981: 239). But it is not Hoggart's program, despite his own leftist progressivism, because he did not presuppose that the decision about what was progressive or fascist came from the judgement of the external critic. Instead, he saw that it might belong to those 'other ways of being in the truth'. In other words, at the root of Hoggart's project is the belief that popular culture can be self-correcting, whether in taste-formation, political progressivism or the emancipation of the imagination. At the root of the position espoused by Hall, Sinfield, Frow and others is the belief that popular culture can only be corrected from without, by intellectuals. This contrasts with Hoggart's *practice* (he did not seek a theory), which sought by critical and educational engagement, both formal and informal, to make popular culture a self-correcting system through practical trial and error.

The only alternative to their own authority that critical and progressive-pessimist intellectuals could see was catastrophe: for instance a descent into an 'anything-goes' celebration of 'populism'. They thought their critical expertise and authority was a bulwark against fascism, which they identified with populism (an *extensio ad absurdum* enthusiastically revived by McGuigan 1992). Thus, Sinfield linked the 'collapse in authority and consensus' with a move to:

> celebrate the equality-of-access, level-playing-field, notion of cultural opportunity that is often imagined in postmodern theory - as

if roaming at will through the Internet and shopping without leaving our IKEA futons will comprise all the freedom that we could reasonably want (Sinfield 1997: xxvii).

Unfortunately, such a tone comes across not as ironic scepticism but as critical self-loathing, turning (unexplained, as if self-evident) hatred of consumerism against the intellectuals themselves, and reducing egalitarianism to self-indulgence. In its pessimism about the uses of digital literacy in a commercial democracy, reducing it to shopping on the internet, it deflects attention away from what 'cultural opportunity', never mind freedom, might look like, preferring the easier option of a 'critical' refusal to engage, based on little more than taste-contempt for affordable DIY furniture. It is a further iteration of the familiar cry of 'more means worse' that has greeted every extension of education, employment and consumer choice, not to mention the franchise, throughout the modern era (Carey 1992; Hartley 2003).

For Sinfield, following a standard line of Marxist cultural materialism, the way out of this impasse - loss of 'authority' on the one hand and lots of 'shopping' on the other - is 'struggle' or socialist agitation. Thus 'struggle' was set up as the high-prestige opposing pole to 'populism'. In this context, Sinfield asked a pertinent question about what postwar British left activism was *for.*

What did we really *intend* - when we cried 'America out', for instance, in Grosvenor Square in 1968? We pushed and shoved at the line of police, with the apparent goal of breaking through and reaching the US Embassy. But what were we going to do when we got there? (Sinfield 1997: xxxii).

This is a good question, one that still applies to street demonstrations, for instance those against globalisation or climate change. Sinfield does not entertain the possibility that the 'intention' was not to achieve an immediate instrumental goal but to achieve self-realisation through theatrical participation in a live social network, participating in a collective drama ritual. This, by the way, is certainly how I experienced the radicalising euphoria of London in 1968. I didn't know Alan Sinfield was in another part of that crowd in Grosvenor Square, but I did know Alan Sinfield - he had been Head Boy of the Royal Wolverhampton Orphan Asylum some years earlier, and I had been his 'fag' (Hartley 1999: 200-3).[1] Doubtless we experienced that day, not to mention that school, in very different ways, but I can answer his question about Grosvenor Square because I was there too, albeit among the 40,000 'milling around' mob, rather than the two- to three-hundred-strong 'get-into-the-Embassy' group (Halloran et al. 1970: 217-18). Although the march opposed British involvement in Vietnam, the event was not only about America. One of those arrested on the day commented: 'I thought it would be a bit of fun ... I don't know anything about politics or Vietnam but I hate coppers.' Another said: 'I think we ought to have more freedom and less control. You can't insult police officers enough' (quoted in Halloran et al. 1970: 79-80). According to a *New Society* survey, two-thirds of those present claimed they were protesting against 'capitalism in general' or against the 'general structure of British society'; or even in favour of 'Home Rule for Wales' (Halloran et al. 1970: 67; 225). In other words, the demonstration was about fellow-feeling among disparate 'we' groups and opposition to a 'they' system. Against the 'status quo' and 'the establishment', it was collectively in favour of change - almost any change.

The demonstration was about how a self might get into a position where individual choices may be determined by the choices of others, by choosing to congregate physically with those others whose choices were valued. It would not necessarily feel like it in the push and shove of the police line, but this rather odd way of putting the matter of 'intention' - of self-actualisation determined by others, and of pleasurable association in the context of serious events - is the foundation of a 'social network market' (Potts et al. 2008), about which more will need to be said later (in Chapter 2). Suffice it to say here that a 'third way' between authority and shopping was and remains available *within* commercial democracies. Self-realisation and intellectual critique are by no means incompatible with popular culture, as the protest songs of the 1960s attested, and the growth of new social movements in that period was fully 'marketised', not least through popular music, countercultural publishing and other creative industries. In short, and as always, the presence of 'struggle' (on the police line) does not imply the absence of 'market' (in the newsagent's shop), nor does the presence of commercial entertainment imply the absence of 'struggle' - especially a struggle for emancipation into intellectual freedom and for connectivity with like-minded others.

## What Is Digital Literacy For?

Fast-forwarding to the contemporary global environment, these issues remain important and unresolved, as Paul Hoggart has observed. However, because of accelerating technological 'affordances' and economic growth since the 1960s, there are now burgeoning possibilities for both professional and popular uses of multimedia, and for both non-market and market-based activism and social network formation. Are these commercialised 'uses of digital literacy' evidence for the progressive potential of self-directed popular agency, or for the success of manipulative corporate populism? Doubtless both of these conditions can be present simultaneously, but the idea that intellectuals can stand aside from the productivity of digital culture can no longer be sustained. It is no longer an option (if it ever was) to criticise popular culture from the outside, because the boundaries between that domain and the domain of formal, intellectual, critical, scientific, journalistic and imaginative knowledge are dissolving. You can *navigate* the online environment to choose social networks or entertainment over science or Project Gutenberg, but these choices are not *structured* by the system, which increasingly allows ordinary people to partake of both popular entertainment and purposeful growth of knowledge simultaneously.

The challenge then is not to oppose populism in the name of some regulatory intellectualism that knows what's good for people, but to capture the energy of 'consumer productivity' itself, and to promote the development of 'consumer entrepreneurship' within a complex system of market-based self-actualisation. Not enough 'critical' attention has been paid to what ordinary people need to learn in order to attain a level of digital literacy appropriate for *producing* as well as *consuming* digital content, thence to participate in the mediated public sphere, to pursue their own private imaginative desires, to contribute to the growth of knowledge, or to develop enterprises and create value (cultural and economic) in commercial and community contexts, not least by scaling up the creative capacity of consumer-users, for instance by linking learning services, local content and national innovation systems. This book takes up the challenge of these developments.

At the heart of this book lies a reappraisal of humanities research and its use in understanding the conditions of a consumer-led society. This is an open, investigative, critical, scientific task (see Chapter 8), as well as an opportunity to engage with creative enterprise and culture. The humanities to date have worked from a dominant intellectual politics that favours 'culture' and the arts over 'mass' media forms, and 'critique' over 'productivity'. Because of a lingering 'media-effects' model that positions audiences as behavioural effects of corporate causation (Gauntlett 1998; 2005), that perspective is sceptical at best about the productive and progressive capacities of the popular audience. Equally, the creativity of the commercial sphere is doubted, and the possibility of achieving intellectual or political freedom in a commercial environment is treated with something close to contempt. These two 'critical' moves confine creativity and productivity to the separate domain of the arts and intellectuals. This approach now needs revisiting in the face of a cultural environment in which innovation arises out of both public and private endeavours (Rifkin 2000: 24-9, 82-95), and out of consumer co-created content or user-led innovation, and not just from the corporate lab. Consumers are influencing and disrupting former patterns of media production and distribution and now 'consumers may gain power through the assertion of new kinds of economic and legal relations and not simply through making meanings' (Jenkins 2004: 36). Now that every user is a publisher, consumption needs to be rethought as action not behaviour, and media consumption as a mode of literacy: that is, an autonomous means of communication in which 'writing' is as widespread as 'reading'; something that was never possible during the era of broadcast, one-to-many, passively received 'mass' communication. The implications are far-reaching, encompassing intellectual debates on the impact of new technologies, the sources, types and outcomes of innovation, and the role of consumer- or user-led innovation, as well as informing policy and industry development in the services sector of the knowledge economy.

In a contested arena there's a need to understand what links opposing viewpoints, such as corporate and community approaches to creativity, to combine critique of power with the promotion of participation - 'creative industries' with 'culture jamming' (Lovink 2003: 204 -16). The industrial era was characterised by concentrations of power based on ownership and control of capital, plant and physical resources. In the creative industries power is concentrated in control over access and distribution of information, resulting in emergent sites of contestation - intellectual property (IP) and copyright law, cyber-democracy, the open source movement and consumer rights. As contemporary cultures transform from the industrial (mass) era of broadcasting and entertainment towards consumer-led interactivity and customisation, there is a need to identify areas where regulation or intervention by state or international authorities is warranted, and where the potential exists to broaden the social base of communications and enterprise, or where increased capacity in semiotic systems resulting from new technologies may encourage new forms of popular literacy in multimedia communications (Jenkins 2003; 2006).

Such an endeavour must also be part of an attempt to

understand longer term changes in knowledge (Lee 2003). Knowledge, culture, communication and consumption are dynamic fields of evolutionary adaptation. They concern the growth of human relationships, values, identities and desires, in complex interaction with the forces of political power, economic and institutional organisation, market coordination and technological invention. Meanings interact with money, economic values with cultural values, the political with the personal. At the 'micro' level of ordinary experience, 'we' both feel and form these forces, interactions and changes as part of the unpredictable immediacy of everyday life. This is exactly the generative 'edge' of growth, but it is rarely experienced at the time as part of a larger pattern. However, larger patterns can be discerned at the 'macro' level of systems and networks, which themselves interconnect and change over time. At this 'macro' scale, it is evident that different aspects of knowledge, culture, communication and identity share important features, and that these amount to a 'paradigm' (in the semiotic rather than the Kuhnian sense) which characterises particular eras. The present period does seem to be one of rapid change, arguably from a 'modern' to a 'global' paradigm (see the table on pages 16 and 17). Richard Hoggart was firmly in the 'modern' paradigm (column 2), but many of the developments he sought to analyse were emergent aspects of the 'global' (column 3). As a result, like most modernist critics, he was apt to judge the emergent paradigm by the values of the then dominant one. Not surprisingly, such a 'parallax error' produced both discomfort in the analyst and bias in the findings. The reappraisal called for in this book, then, seeks to investigate the dynamics of the 'global' paradigm from 'within', as it were.

## The value chain of meanings: the ascribed source of meaning in different epochs in the modernising West

| Era: | 1 Pre-modern | 2 Modern | 3 Global |
|---|---|---|---|
| **Value chain . . .** | | | |
| *. . . of merchandise* | origination/ production | commodity/ distribution | consumption/ use |
| *. . . of meaning* | author/producer | text/ performance | reader/ audience |
| **When, where, who (time, place, population)** | | | |
| *When* | medieval | modern | global |
| *Where* | church | public sphere | private life |
| *Who (population)* | the faithful | the public | DIY citizen |
| *Who (intermediary)* | priest | publisher | marketing |
| **How (regime)** | | | |
| *Theorist* | Bible | Marx | Foucault |
| *Subjectivity* | soul | individual(ism) | experience |
| *Power-base* | pain of death/ hell | war | administration of life |
| *Sovereignty* | monarch/divine | nation-state | self |
| *Arms-bearer* | knight/crusader | conscript/ volunteer | terrorist |
| *Enemy* | peer/heretic | country | civilian |
| *State* | 'Hobbesian' | 'Machiavellian' | 'Kantian' |
| **Why (knowledge)** | | | |
| *Philosophy* | revelation | scarcity | plenty |
| *Epistemology* | theology | empiricism | plebiscite |
| *Educational reach* | elite | mass | universal |

| What (form) | | | |
|---|---|---|---|
| *Interpretive form* | exegesis ('Q')[2] | criticism (Leavis/Hoggart) | redaction |
| *Creative form* | ritual/liturgy | realism (science/journalism/novel) | reality (TV) |
| **What *for* (communicative politics)** | | | |
| *Mode of literacy* | hear only | read only | read/write |
| *Mode of address* | convert | convince (campaign) | converse |
| **Who says (choice control)** | | | |
| *Source of control* | 'Him' – divine | 'Them' – expert | 'Me' – self |
| *Source of choices* | no choices | publisher/provider | navigator/aggregator |
| **Agent of knowledge** | cleric | reading public/media audience | 'consumer entrepreneurs' |
| | = Fundamentalism | = Modernism | = Globalisation |

From John Hartley (2008a), *Television Truths: Forms of Knowledge in Popular Culture,* Blackwell, Oxford, p. 28; and see John Hartley (2004a), 'The "value chain of meaning" and the new economy', *International Journal of Cultural Studies,* 7(1), pp. 129-41.

## Multimedia Literacy - Print, Media, Critical, Digital

After half a century, what are the implications of Richard Hoggart's *Uses of Literacy* for educational reform, in the light of subsequent changes from 'read only' literacy to 'read-write' uses of multimedia? I argue that a broad extension of popular literacy via consumer-created digital content offers not only emancipationist potential in line with Hoggart's own project of critical citizenship-formation but also economic benefits via the dynamics of creative innovation.

Multimedia 'popular entertainments' pose a challenge

to formal education, but not in the way that Hoggart feared. Instead of producing 'tamed helots' (Hoggart 1957: 205), commercial culture may be outpacing formal schooling in promoting creative digital literacy via entrepreneurial and distributed learning. It may indeed be that those in need of a creative makeover are not teenagers but teachers. If we do live in a commercial but humane democracy, as Richard Hoggart fervently hoped that we would, then the popular media are a chief means for interconnecting both the human and the democratic parts of the community, and for linking experts and specialists in government, business and the professions to the general population of 'ordinary people'. As is well known, Hoggart thought that the 'commercial' part was getting out of step with the 'humane' part, to say nothing of the 'democratic'. Commercially catered entertainments seemed to be propagating a new form of literacy - purposeless, consumptive, selfish - that was out of step with both the goals of formal schooling and the home and class culture of the industrialised working population. Hoggart was among the first to think about how commercial entertainment intersects with and extends formal literacy, and how that might affect culture and citizenship. In *The Uses of Literacy* he wrote mostly about popular printed materials. He didn't consider radio or cinema at all, and only addressed the 'uses of television' in 1960, when he published an article in *Encounter* under that title (Hoggart 1960; and see Hartley 1999). Since then, it may be argued that popular media have evolved not once but twice, first through television (1950s to 1970s) and then via interactive and online media (since the Clinton administration). The latter have also been at the forefront of a rapid acceleration in information technology, consumerism and globalisation.

Thus, half a century after *The Uses of Literacy*, it seems timely for a new attempt to be made to understand these forces in relation to the *uses* to which both lay populations and expert elites put their 'media literacy'.

One important change since Hoggart's day is the extent to which media literacy itself has evolved from 'read-only' (broadcast, one-to-many) to 'read and write' (interactive, peer-to-peer). Early media theorists compared broadcasting to the pulpit or soap-box, where a single message was shouted from the perspective of some institutional vested interest. The role of the populace was to stand around passively and soak it up. However, in the last few years and at gathering pace, non-professionals have taken up these media as an autonomous means of communication for themselves. 'Writing' is catching up with 'reading'. Here media literacy is merely following the historical pattern set by print literacy. In the early modern period the use of reading spread well before that of writing, and even if people could write, they tended not to have much use for that skill in everyday intercourse and commerce. Only when a significant proportion of people at large began to write as well as read (around two-thirds of adults) did Western society produce journalism, the Enlightenment, the Industrial Revolution, the novel and democracy. It was at that point that the social activists and emancipationists of the day realised what a friend they had in literacy, and so began the long haul to invest in it sufficiently, via public schooling and private propagation, for everyone to be a participant, and for the skill to be put to useful ends. Ever since, 'universal' print literacy has been a measure of advanced status for any country wanting to compete in the modern world.

In contrast, when the electronic (broadcast) media got

going during the first half of the twentieth century, the intelligentsia were under the influence of high modernism on the
cultural side and the spectre of demagogic totalitarianism
on the political side. It was a climate in which few policy
activists thought that a new 'literacy' was at hand, much less
one that needed to be taught. Instead, following Adorno, they
thought that ordinary people needed to be armed against the
influence of such media, which were seen as a threat to print
literacy and the rational and imaginative values it was said to
promote. Just as no special training beyond native curiosity
and scepticism was needed for people to appreciate stage
shows or listen to sermons, so the new world of entertainment
and persuasion (both political and commercial) seemed to
need no special literacy. If it was involved at all, it needed
to be a 'critical literacy', dedicated to counteracting rather
than extending the reach and sway of what were thought to
be powerful and unscrupulous forces acting upon the people.
This is what was taught in schools: not how to make the most
of the electronic media but how to make the least of them. It
did not occur to many commentators that the general run of
humanity might use these new media as they used a pencil
or their own voice to express their own identity, relationships
and ideas. Those who did think about the emancipationist
potential of radio and cinema, like Berthold Brecht (1979/80),
Humphrey Jennings (1985) or Hans Magnus Enzensberger
(1997), tended to think about media literacy in class terms
rather than personal ones: the 'masses' could represent
themselves via new media, but mainly *as* masses.

   With the popularisation of online media in affluent economies, we need to extend the notion of 'media literacy' beyond
the defensive notion of 'critical reading' and 'media literacy'

as taught in schools, towards what ought to be called 'digital literacy' — a form of hands-on productive expression, taught by and within the milieu in which it is deployed, using multi-platform devices to 'write' as well as 'read' electronic media. As this capability edges towards the two-thirds level at which print literacy achieved its most dynamic cultural and political effects, there has been little call for the kind of investment in its propagation - not to mention its uses - that accompanied print literacy. Digital literacy is primarily taught on a 'peer to peer', informal basis. The investment is almost all private, seeking to develop markets rather than citizens. It is a 'demand-side' rather than a 'supply-side' model of literacy-propagation, and for that very reason it has attracted less attention than it warrants from educational and cultural thinkers, who tend to cluster around publisher/provider models and not to know enough about how digital literacy is learnt (by doing) in informal contexts or how it is used among untutored populations.

Richard Hoggart thought that the popular uses of print literacy were largely purposeless, even wasteful - they amounted to 'abuses' - and he was even less enamoured of such self-taught 'media literacy' as he encountered; for example his famously dim view of youthful taste in popular (American) music. Now, digital literacy too is developing apace in a commercial environment, largely for non-instrumental purposes - self-expression, relationship-maintenance, communication, entertainment. Should it be taken up in formal public education more systematically than it has been? What might that contribute to a humane but commercial democracy? Or should we take a dim view of the whole shebang?

After its invention and technical propagation throughout Europe and across the world - a process that took a mere century from the 1450s to the 1550s in a universe without paved roads - print literacy remained for a time largely tied to instrumental purposes: religion (ideology), commerce, government (control). That gap between elite and lay populations was marked by a difference between those who could and did read and write for all purposes including personal expression, on the one hand, and the larger population who were taught a 'read-only' version of print literacy. They could read but did not write, especially not for publication. At a societal level print literacy was geared to the needs of closed expert systems: clerical, scientific, governmental, commercial. It was rarely used by 'ordinary' folk for leisure consumption (let alone production), personal expression, the maintenance of communities of interest, or for the life of the imagination ('literature'). One of the purposes of instrumental print literacy was modernisation itself; to such an extent that influential commentators saw political democracy as a 'consequence' of literacy (Goody & Watt 1963).

At the same time, however, it was the popular media - not formal education - that began to fill the gap between elites and popular readerships with non-instrumental read-only literacy. The plain-folk got sensationalism (both radical and commercial) along with their science and sermons. In other words, and more accurately, a demand-led element was established in the economy of literacy, in addition to the existing supply-side provision. Hoggart was the first to notice that these demand-led uses of literacy were both quite different from expert or instrumental uses and also worthy of serious inquiry. Hoggart was interested in mass entertainment from the point of view of the popular readership. Famously, he found it wanting, at odds with self-made working-class culture. That is why his work is associated with the valorisation of 'critical literacy', which means an astute readership. Critical literacy was thought to be emancipationist, to allow for independent thought and active participation: 'critical' popular readers may turn into activists, or novelists.

In Hoggart's time, the era of one-way, broadcast communication and supply-side providers, there was little room for a popular uptake of *publishing*. The broadcast media failed completely to promote published writing among wide sections of their newly acquired mass readership. So the lag between reading and writing remained. People could enjoy stories, but not tell their own. Popular self-publication can now be contemplated, however, because the era of one-way 'read-only' media of mass and broadcast communication is transforming into the interactive era of 'read-write' multimedia. The shift from print via broadcasting to multimedia raises the 'Hoggart question' for the era of the internet: what are the cultural, non-instrumental uses of multimedia literacy?'

## Repurposing Education for Innovation

In current business, economic and policy discourse, innovation and especially creative innovation is the general-purpose or enabling process that will maintain international competitiveness for advanced countries and firms, and accelerate developing countries' progress towards prosperity; so goes the argument. The rhetoric that is used in these contexts to describe the *innovative entrepreneur* is exactly that which has been used throughout modernity to describe the *creative artist*. Artists have long been habituated to working with risk, intuition and constant change. The cultural sector has been 'constantly innovative, anticipating and responding to the market through an intuitive immersion into the field, willing to break the rules, going beyond the 9-5, thriving on risk and failure, mixing work and life, meaning and money - this was a cutting edge sector which the others could look to as a model' (O'Connor & Gu 2006: 273-4). In other words, *artists* became the template for *entrepreneurs,* and creative enterprise the model for the new economy.

Culture shifts from its position as a sphere of opposition to the modernising fury of commercial enterprise (critique), to become a vital component in a country's competitiveness (productivity). Suddenly, it seems, people at the humanities end of the academic spectrum may prove to be directly useful in the wealth-creating forums of business and government. And so, the wider question now is: if enterprise needs the creativity of the artist, and if innovation needs the 'literacy' of both the intellectual and an astute reading public, how widely among the general or ordinary population can such capabilities be distributed? As for educational institutions, what role might they play in promoting the use of digital technologies for intellectual and creative emancipation among whole populations? How might they assist in scaling up that usage to benefit the innovation system? Or should that be done by the private sector, with just-in-time (sink or swim) 'training' for creative entrepreneurs and commercial pay-as-you-learn for the creative citizen? If the situation is left to develop haphazardly and commercially as it has already begun to unfold, the question of what universities are for will become more insistent and uncomfortable as distributed learning takes hold outside of formal education institutions.

At the conclusion *of The Uses of Literacy* Richard Hoggart remarks that 'it seems unlikely' that 'a majority of any class will have strongly intellectual pursuits'. Recognising this, his recipe for action is not to try to turn people into intellectuals, getting workers to read *The Times* rather than the tabloids (Hoggart 1957: 281). His objection to popular entertainments is not that they fail to recruit workers to the intelligentsia, but that they 'make it harder for people without an intellectual bent to become wise in their own way'. If that is the goal, is it still true that the popular media make it harder, in the era of YouTube, MySpace, Flickr and Wikipedia?

If innovation and creativity are the hope of commercial democracies, then it may be necessary to ask even more ambitious questions than those posed by the desire to educate a critically literate population. Indeed, these are the contemporary 'uses of Richard Hoggart': to investigate what *ought to be hoped for* in the currently unfolding phase of audiovisual literacy. Do contemporary interactive media constitute just such another way of 'being in the truth', and would massive public, private and personal investment in developing creative imaginative talents within a reformed educational infrastructure make a contribution not only to the inner life of individuals but also to the wealth of nations? Is the emancipation of the individual into intellectual and creative freedom also the royal road to economic improvement?

The same question can be posed the other way around. Underlying the economic and educational arguments is a commitment to the inner life of individual imagination - it is the source of creativity and of knowledge. This means that economic policy based on existing structures (the market) or institutions (like the firm) is not enough; it simply reinvents the past. Innovation policy requires that we enable agents to think for themselves about what they want to do. Economic policy needs to focus on 'another way of being in the truth' - namely that individuals drive innovation through the spread and increase of knowledge. The individual remains the 'unit' of creativity, no matter what scale is achieved in distribution or sales, and notwithstanding that individual creativity rarely gets very far on its own (it needs to work in teams).

If we buy the argument that contemporary economies are complex adaptive innovation networks driven by myriad individual agents - rather than closed expert systems that can be controlled by elite institutions or leaderships - then the question arises of how to encourage individual imagination within a complex network. One way to think about this question is to focus on the figure who will take the system into the future as both agent and object of structural change: 'the teenager'. This is the very group that Richard Hoggart encountered in milk-bars, to his own dismay. His teens were objects: 'the directionless and tamed helots of a machine-minding class' (1957: 205). He missed the opportunity to value these denizens of the milk-bars as *agents* for the R&D they were all too visibly pursuing as he watched, via juke box, clothes, dance movements, looks and Americanisms. This was the 'larval' stage - dumb, receptive, greedily gathering resources - of what pupated in due course to 'adult' productivity as these teenagers became the entrepreneurs of 1960s pop culture and counterculture. Given Hoggart's preference for existing structure (self-made working-class culture) over dynamic change (American pop market), then what's needed is not a simple application of 'Hoggart' to current phenomena, but an argument for contemporary Hoggartians not to make the same mistake again, and to recognise that there are indeed 'other ways of being in the truth'. What looks like aimless time-wasting, daydreaming and mischief to the institutionalised expert should also be seen (or at least investigated) as an 'incubator' in which future creative possibilities are growing.

The gap between home, work and school where young people in particular can think about identity, mix with peers, express their own thoughts and escape some of the structures of social control, also underlies popular entertainment, live and mediated, driving the imaginative content of the most important of the creative industries. Music, media and games are the 'industrial', scaled-up form taken by adolescent daydreaming (narratives of wish-fulfilment) and peer-group mischief (play, games or action-conflict drama). The popular media have grown up in the gap between elite systems (of government and business) and general populations, giving highly capitalised expression to people's 'inner life' desires and fears, wishes and conflicts, plots and games.

Normally government is devoted only to controlling or at least minimising such tendencies. But teenagers seem in opposition to parental or institutional control only because the latter are 'maps of the past' while the teenager is intuitively oriented to the future. Public policy needs to think of the daydreaming mischievous teenager not as a threat but as an opportunity, even though actual manifestations of teenage-led creative innovation may not always present such a pretty sight. As Hoggart (1957) put it:

> The hedonistic but passive barbarian who rides a fifty-horse-power bus for threepence to see a five-million-dollar film for one-and-eightpence, is not simply a social oddity; he is a portent (205).

Portents are harbingers of change - teenager demand drives creative innovation. Hoggart disliked the extent to which young people's dreams were being dreamed for them by the entertainment industry (although he didn't mind if it was done by Auden or Lawrence). That is still an issue, as it has been since at least Shakespeare, despite the massive increase in youthful self-expression made possible via consumer-generated content. However, even when facilitated by entertainment producers or 'killer apps' designed by adults, the teenager is still the 'unit' of demand for and expression of change, just as the individual is the 'unit' for creative innovation. It was exactly this that worried Hoggart about teenagers, his purpose being to describe what he wanted to call 'an ugly change' (Owen 2005: 171) that threatened the 'order of existence' (Hoggart 1957: 69) that he valued. For a later reappraisal of his 'method', perhaps it is sufficient to notice that he exercises detailed observational acuity in identifying cultural change and showing how the tension between order and change is keenly felt and culturally productive in its own right. It may indeed be necessary *not* to follow Hoggart's own particular evaluations, which seem to value working-class family disputes and even household suicides (67-9) higher than milk-bar decor and 'juke-box boys' (203-4). Such preferences get in the way of recognising that the *cultural* tension between order and change, personified in the 'juke-box boys' themselves, is not a choice (when pushed, Hoggart chose order) but is itself a driver and generator of creative innovation. He recognises this in the implicit contrast between 'tamed helots' and creative imagination. How can a country avoid the former and encourage the latter?

## Educating Teachers

Education systems will ignore the lesson of consumer-led, distributive, iterative and multi-sourced learning at their peril, as will broadcasters and publishers. These 'other ways of being in the truth' are perhaps the best hope yet that the 'truly concrete and personal' expression that underlies Hoggart's vision for 'the quality of life, the kind of response, the rootedness in wisdom and maturity' within 'popular art' can be achieved by a wide spectrum of creative citizens around the world, with the surprising extra innovation that such expression is itself the R&D component of a creative economy, contributing to the growth of knowledge and progress of society.

Can the effort to modernise and repurpose higher education extend to schooling too?[3] This is a tricky issue, since one part of schooling is dedicated to 'taming' the 'helots'; it is therefore the very environment from which many teenagers wish to escape, using their own untutored multimedia literacy to enjoy their own imaginative universe, where their private daydreams can be elaborated with the aid of a corporate soundtrack (the iPod) and with stories of wish-fulfilment (movies), their fears expressed in songs of angst and romance, and their own stratagems for mischief and peer-bonding advanced by means of various mobile devices from the Walkman to the iPhone. This disconnect - perhaps amounting to a structural contradiction - between formal schooling and informal acculturation has given rise, in turn, to public anxiety about what teens are up to. Just to give a typical case in point, in 2004 the *Australian Financial Review* (Australia's version of the *Financial Times)* ran a long feature called 'The Secret Life of Teens'. It suggested that what happens on the other side of the bedroom door in the family home today, where fourteen-year-olds hold electronic court via mobile, modem and media, is literally a closed world to parents and other grown-ups:

> Australian teenagers today are the most electronically savvy, the most educated and the most globally aware generation ever. They have money, they are pragmatic about studying hard and getting a job and they are optimistic. They are the 'click and go' generation, they live in democratised families, they negotiate and they feel entitled to privacy (20).

Teens are perennially fascinating objects of speculation in the serious media as well as the popular media, because their 'secret life' represents in concrete form the potential shape of the future for everyone. Their lives may not be such a secret after all, but the realities of the world they are facing - *their* futures - may indeed remain hidden from the sight and imagination of some of those whose job it is to worry about them, including parents, journalists, educators, policy-makers and elected representatives. If today's teens do live in a world that is barely recognisable to some of those professionals, it is important to share the secret. However, it may not be easy to share the secret *in school.* Teenagers are used to teachers seeking to control, minimise and render 'useful' their digital literacy. They don't necessarily think that's what school is for. So it is not a simple matter of deciding to teach digital literacy in schools as we currently know them. To make a worthwhile contribution to the further development of digital literacy, schools will need to change themselves just as much as they seek to change teenagers. The main thing that needs to change in schools is ... teachers.

## Creative Workforce

In seeking to identify the driver of social and economic advancement during the present century, John Howkins argues that IT alone is no longer enough. He suggests that the 'information society' is already beginning to give way to something much more challenging:

> If I was a bit of data I would be proud of living in an information society. But as a thinking, emotional, creative being - on a good day, anyway - I want something better. We need information. But we also need to be active, clever, and persistent in challenging this information. We need to be original, sceptical, argumentative, often bloody-minded and occasionally downright negative - in one word, creative (Howkins 2002).

The sociologist of occupations Richard Florida has identified what he sees as a new economic class - the 'creative class' - that he argues will dominate economic and cultural life in the century to come, just as the working class predominated in the earlier decades of the twentieth century and the service class has since then. While the creative class is smaller than the service class, it is nevertheless the dynamo of growth and change for services and thence the economy as a whole, and incidentally for the temper of the times too - it's a cultural and social force as well as an economic one. 'Classes' have migrated, as it were, from blue-collar and white-collar environments to the 'no-collar' workplace:

> Artists, musicians, professors and scientists have always set their own hours, dressed in relaxed and casual clothes and worked in stimulating environments. They could never be forced to work, yet

they were never truly not at work. With the rise of the Creative Class, this way of working has moved from the margins to the economic mainstream (Florida 2002: 12-13).

Florida describes how the no-collar workplace 'replaces traditional hierarchical systems of control with new forms of self-management, peer-recognition and pressure and intrinsic forms of motivation', which he calls 'soft control'. Thus:

> In this setting, we strive to work more independently and find it much harder to cope with incompetent managers and bullying bosses. We trade job security for autonomy. In addition to being fairly compensated for the work we do and the skills we bring, we want the ability to learn and grow, shape the content of our work, control our own schedules and express our identities through work (13).

## Creative Educators?

The industrial organisation of workforces with strong unionisation leads to standardisation of work experience. When the employer is a command bureaucracy, as are many education authorities, then control, predictability and due process will always prevail over innovation, risk and customisation. Even their own organisations recognise that teachers are trained for something other than 'fostering creativity':

> To date, the fostering of creativity and of innovation in school students has not itself been a major focus of [teachers'] professional learning activity . . . These are very substantial challenges (MCEETYA 2003: 163-4).

Sir Ken Robinson makes the connection between economic and educational imperatives:

> The economic circumstances in which we all live, and in which our children will have to make their way, are utterly different from those of 20 or even 10 years ago. For these we need different styles of education and different priorities. We cannot meet the challenges of the 21st century with the educational ideologies of the 19th. Our own times are being swept along on an avalanche of innovations in science, technology, and social thought. To keep pace with these changes, or to get ahead of them, we will need our wits about us - literally. We must learn to be creative (Robinson 2001: 200-3).

David Hargreaves says that 'the time is ripe for exploring new ways in which to increase teachers' professional knowledge and skill'. He argues the need for 'deep change' that will *transform* rather than simply *improve* schools. That need is driven by:

> The growing recognition that in a knowledge-based economy more people need to be more creative and this in itself will require new approaches to teaching. Without reducing the importance of the basics, we must now aspire to nurture through education the qualities of creativity, innovativeness and enterprise (Hargreaves 2003: 3-4).

For themselves as professionals and for their students, teachers need to:

• nurture the individual talent that will win employment

- develop in students the skills to manage a portfolio career - self-employed, freelance, casual or part-time, not with a single employer or even industry
- learn project management and entrepreneurship as core skills
- encourage project-based work in teams with multiple partners who change over time
- connect to an international environment where continuing education is normal
- increasingly prioritise life-design as well as employment skills
- learn - for themselves as well as for their students - how to navigate from entry-level workforce jobs to wealth-creating destinations, which may include giving up employment and working independently.

All these objectives require major changes in disciplinary knowledge, pedagogy, curriculum, assessment and the experience of education for both educators and students. Each of them is a 'life' skill rather than 'literacy', digital or otherwise. But all of them are required if digital literacy is to flourish across a wide population.

## Learning as a Distributed System

The starting point for renewing the public sector must be a renewal of its relationship with the society it serves. Ministers should be held accountable for solving problems which electors want solved, not running government departments (Leadbeater 1999: 207, 215).

Charles Leadbeater's strong warning about the perils of business-as-usual management, rather than tackling emergent problems, applies directly to the challenges facing those who promote learning within a knowledge society. Public education systems (including the independent schools sector) are not necessarily best placed to respond to the challenge of the new knowledge economy and the need for innovative, creative, adaptive and curious consumer-citizens to make it prosper.

Twentieth-century educational modernisation, based first on massively expanding formal institutions and more recently on increasing their productivity with centrally regulated performance targets, has certainly strengthened the education *system* of schools, universities and government departments. But inadvertently it has had a negative effect both on the kind of knowledge imparted and on the wider social desire to learn, because it has snuck the industrial-era 'closed expert system' into the education 'industry' at exactly the moment when 'industry' itself is evolving towards a market-based open innovation network:

> This approach to modernization also reinforces a deeply conservative approach to education, as a body of knowledge imparted by organizations with strong hierarchies and demarcated professional disciplines ... Two traditions are reflected in this culture: the monasteries, which were closed repositories for knowledge in the form of precious manuscripts, and Taylor's factory, which encouraged standardized, easily replicated knowledge. The result is a system that is a curious hybrid of factory, sanctuary, library and prison (Leadbeater 1999: 110).

Instead *of providing* disciplinary knowledge in a controlled environment, Leadbeater argues that education should tip over to the demand side; it needs to inspire the *desire to learn:*

> The point of education should not be to inculcate a body of knowledge, but to develop capabilities: the basic ones of literacy and numeracy as well as the capability to act responsibly towards others, to take initiative and to work creatively and collaboratively. The most important capability, and one which traditional education is worst at creating, is the ability and yearning to carry on learning. Too much schooling kills off the desire to learn (1999: 111).

Merely expanding the formal education system is not the direction to take for creating a society characterised by 'yearning for learning':

> We need hybrid public and private institutions and funding structures. Schools and universities should become more like hubs of learning, within the community, capable of extending into the community (Leadbeater 1999: 111-12).

Individuals and families can and will take more responsibility for their own knowledge needs. Learning services will be provided by private as well as public institutions, for purposes determined by the needs of the learners themselves rather than for formal accreditation and certification. In short, *learning will become a distributed system,* dedicated to creativity, innovation, customised needs and networked across many sites from the family kitchen to the business breakfast as well as the classroom and workplace. Educational practices in the various systems need to open up, to become more permeable and responsive to changing economic and social factors. The model for distributed learning for an open innovation network has already been promulgated in the shape of online and mobile media.

The shift from teaching as *transmission* of knowledge to learning as *production* of knowledge means that an important responsibility for the system will be helping people learn to learn and to become motivated to learn. In this scenario, teachers become *learning entrepreneurs,* managers or producers, and teaching gives way to the design of learning programs. This is not just a shift in the lexicon but a transformation of practice. If the purpose of education systems is to prepare young people in appropriate ways for the challenges and responsibilities they will face throughout their lives, and if society is changing, 'so should the way in which we introduce young people to it' (Bentley 1998: 38).

## Learning Entrepreneurs

Richard Hoggart was evidently not persuaded that the university as he knew it was adapted to the task of analysing, let alone promoting, desirable uses of literacy by working consumers. So when he went to Birmingham it was to set up something quite novel among the universities of the day, the Centre for Contemporary Cultural Studies. He continued to work through non-canonical educational institutions like the WEA, UNESCO and Goldsmiths, and to intervene in educational aspects of commercial culture (e.g. the *Chatterley* trial and the Pilkington Report). His example may still be instructive, and not only at the level of tertiary education. Hoggart was a learning entrepreneur, seeking to develop the uses of literacy among the industrial workforce and popular consumers; to make them 'critical' - by which he meant 'creative' and 'innovative' as well as independent-minded, although the lexicon of the times differed. His important innovation - made against the grain of his own left-Leavisite and somewhat anti-American cultural prejudices - was to understand that popular literacy is not only a matter of formal education; it is also a matter of culture, and that such a culture was decisively shaped by commercial media that young people enjoyed in their 'free' time. A distributed, entertainment-hungry 'reading public' was already an important component of 'commercial democracies' in the 1950s. With the subsequent acceleration of celebrity culture, the 'economy of attention' (Lanham 2006) and peer-to-peer or DIY creative content-creation using digital technologies, the horizons of that public have been radically expanded: now, at least in principle, every reader-consumer can also be a publisher, a journalist and a 'creative'. Hoggart wanted ordinary people and non-intellectual populations to be able to make the best of their literacy, to 'become wise in their own way'. I see Hoggart as a 'theorist' of literacy and moderniser of the 'idea of the university' (Newman 1907), as well as a founder of cultural studies (which was but the vehicle for this deeper purpose: Hoggart 1992: 26). He was an emancipationist of the imagination and of the intellect, and that explains the continuing 'uses of Richard Hoggart'. The question that faces his successors is whether it is schools, teachers and intellectuals rather than popular media and consumer services that pose the greater threat to the realisation of those 'other ways of being in the truth' that he valued.

*'Generatively-enabled activity by amateurs can
lead to results that would not have been
produced by a firm-mediated market model.'*
Jonathan Zittrain (2008: 84)


# 2

# From the Consciousness Industry to the Creative Industries
## Consumer-created Content, Social Network Markets and the Growth of Knowledge

### Media Industry Studies: All Change?

According to *Time* magazine (25 December), 2006 was a tipping point: the year of *'you* as in YouTube, the year of consumer-created content. If this was a new reality for the media industries themselves, what did it mean for media and cultural studies? The field is overdue for a consumer makeover. For too long it has been dominated by top-down, ideologically motivated political-economy approaches that have preserved the media-effects paradigm ('what do media do to audiences?') well beyond its use-by date. In studies of media industries, too much attention has been paid to providers and firms, too little to consumers and markets. But with user-created content, the question first posed more than a generation ago by the uses and gratifications method, and taken up by semiotics and the active audience tradition ('what do audiences do with media?'), has resurfaced with renewed

39

force. What is new is that where this question - of what the media industries and audiences did with each other - used to be individualist and functionalist, now, with the advent of social networks using Web 2.0 affordances, it can be re-posed at the level of systems and populations as well.

There is also new hope for integrating the study of economic and cultural systems and processes, which histori-cally have been addressed by different academic disciplines. Now there is a chance to bring together, perhaps for the first time in a thoroughgoing way, the political-economy and text/audience traditions, to unify the study of economic and cultural values in the process of formation and change.

The industriousness of 'amateur' creative users suggests that self-made media content has already disrupted the expert paradigm that dominated media production during the broadcast era. Is this a portent for industry in general? If so, then the YouTube generation is modelling the future of innovation and growth across the economy, and beyond into cultural and community contexts. In that case, 'media industry studies' would provide a general public service if it were to devote itself to understanding emergent systems and values, both cultural and economic; if it focused on analysing the process and dynamics of change directly. Such changes are leading the field beyond the study of 'media power' towards that of the 'growth of knowledge'.

However, there remains a strong trace of ideological stand-off in much work on media industries: the pro-business spruikers of innovation (e.g. Beinhocker 2006; Leadbeater 2002, 2006) versus the anti-capitalist sceptics (e.g. Garnham 1990; Schiller 1989). Continuing problems carry through from the industrial or expert paradigm to the consumer or social-network paradigm, and new problems demand urgent attention. These include both monopolistic tendencies (e.g. one supplier of content) and monopsonic tendencies (e.g. one buyer of labour) among existing and new media corporations, and the growing issue of 'free labour' - the work put in by consumers and users as well as the conditions of employment in 'media industries' (Terranova 2000). Nevertheless, such problems are not well understood using a technology of critique (as it were) that is based on *industry;* what's needed instead is one attuned to *information.* But taking this step changes the critical rules. As Tiziana Terranova (2004) puts it: 'The cultural politics of information is no radical alternative that springs out of a negativity to confront a monolithic social technology of power. It is rather a *positive feedback effect* of informational cultures as such.'

The standard 'critical' stance - 'negativity to confront monolithic . . . power' - reminds us that the glass of media participation remains stubbornly half-empty. But it fails to account for how it came to be half-full. Critical analysis need not take sides, whether the slogan is Google's 'you can make money without doing evil',[1] or News Corp's simpler - and here I paraphrase - 'let's monetise that'! To dismiss both new-media developments and their marketisation is not only 'critical' short-sightedness, it is also 'industrial' suicide, as Peter Chernin, president and chief operating officer of News Corporation, has pointed out to his industry colleagues:

'There are huge rewards for those who innovate, and death to those who do not,' he said . . . According to Chernin, traditional media companies had to take notice of technological developments and adapt their business model accordingly. The knee-jerk reaction is to take pot-shots at what you don't understand. To dismiss user-generated content as crap and blogs as unauthoritative is not only unproductive but a waste of time,' Chernin claimed (Advanced-television.com 2007).[2]

So 'media industry studies' needs a critical makeover, one that is forced on it by changes in the external environment, both intellectual and industrial. It needs curiosity about change and growth, not an insistence on (rigid) structure and (residual) power.

## Industry: Reality or Metaphor?

The problem lies not with the laudable effort to *study* 'industries' but with the term 'industry' itself. In common with language in general, the social sciences and the humanities share a long history of borrowing metaphors from other domains to identify and describe their own object of study. 'Industry' is one such term. However, like other metaphors of organisational scale - 'capitalism', 'society', 'culture', 'globalisation' - the name itself does not describe a necessary empirical fact on the ground. You can't stub your toe on an industry. Perhaps this is why in economics, a discipline that does have ambitions towards scientific and mathematical exactitude, 'industry' is a derived term not a natural category:

> In microeconomic theory industries do not exist. What exists, of course, are agents, prices, commodities, firms, transactions, markets, organizations, technologies and institutions. These are economically real at the level of any individual agent's transformations or transactions (Potts et al. 2008).

Firms produce goods or services, while 'industries' are abstract aggregations of firms, actions, prices and the rest. 'Industry' is often used even more loosely, interchangeably with business, trade, market, or even community, as in 'do you work in the industry?'[3] This doesn't mean that the term is useless or a lie; it means that it must be used with care, carrying with it a full trail of analytical explanation. But instead, media studies imported it as self-evident and as real, with connotations that endowed vertically integrated industrial corporations not only with moral qualities (chiefly evil) but also with exorbitant or 'fabulous powers', as Ian Connell pointed out a generation ago (Connell 1984). As a result, 'the industry' - that is, the media - is frequently described as having properties it cannot possess, for instance consciousness, which in turn are soon personalised into barons, moguls and assorted betes noir - Hearst, Berlusconi, Murdoch . . . Citizen Kane . . . stage villain. In general, the metaphor of industrial-scale agency carries with it connotations of power, control, hidden agendas and the objectification of the consumer/audience, often provoking moralistic or ideological misgivings about wealth-creation *per se*.

'Industry' is a modern term. Pre-modern and traditional societies did not have a word for it. It is borrowed from the Latin for 'diligence', of the kind frequently attributed to ants. It originated in early modern English (in the 1500s) to describe individual actions: 'intelligent or clever working; skill, ingenuity, dexterity, or cleverness in doing anything' *(Oxford English Dictionary)*. In the nineteenth century it was applied metaphorically to large-scale systematic productive work and manufacture (as in 'Captains of Industry'; an Industrialist); and in the twentieth century it was applied metaphorically

again, to any 'profitable practice' ('the Shakespeare industry', 'the abortion industry') or to the industrialisation of a
country (these examples are from the OED).

This extrapolation, from individual 'studied diligence' to
the Industrial Revolution and thence to 'organised exploitation',
brought with it a model of a system. 'Industry' henceforth
required more than individual industriousness. The *system*
couldn't work without spare money (capital),[4] specialisation
(division of labour), coal and steam (new sources of energy),
railways and Reuters (faster communications), the cotton jenny
(technology and machinery), manufactories and cities ('industrial' scale), the proletariat (an organised and disciplined labour
force) and their wives (increasingly affluent consumers). Individual craftsmen were reduced to 'labour', their value to that
of 'hands', and work itself was changed from being handiwork
to repetitive routines, as satirised in Charlie Chaplin's *Modern
Times* (1936). The twentieth century was marked by continuing
ideological adversarialism, 'class war' in intellectual as well as
industrial life, and so the concept of 'industry' as a system never
travelled far without this baggage. It was just such a vision of
industrialisation that was in the minds of those intellectuals,
critics and sociologists who contemplated what was called
the 'consciousness *industry*' and the '*industrialisation* of the
mind' (Enzensberger 1974), or the '*manufacture* of consent'
(Herman & Chomsky 1988). When it came to 'the media',
therefore, it was almost inevitable that 'industry' meant not
'studied diligence' in the production and dissemination of
meaningful representations but 'organised exploitation' on
a society-wide scale, using bias, manipulation and ideology
rather than creativity, innovation and dialogue.

Most of what goes on in the media 'industries' (as in any other

service) is not captured in the industrial idea of the 'production of goods'. This is another extended metaphor. Media
'content' is not a 'good'; consumption is not what media audiences do. 'Consumption' is in fact a pre-industrial, agricultural
metaphor, appropriate to foodstuffs that are literally consumed.
Cultural or symbolic 'goods', like music, screen narratives
or printed stones, remain alive for indefinite reconsumption
(Garnham 1987; Lotman 1990). Furthermore, the 'industry'
label is not accurate for small or micro-businesses that drive
the creation of novel content. Many performers and freelanc-
ers are more like itinerant traders than industrialists; Terranova
(2004) dubs the open-source movement 'Internet tinkers'. They
operate in a 'market' where the real 'consumer' to date has been
none other than the pre-internet monopsonic 'media industries'.
Musicians sell to record labels, moviemakers to film distributors, TV producers to networks. Creatives are organised into a
market that services giant corporations. One result of this is a
persistent tendency among the general public to treat creative IP
as a public good, resulting in the fascinating and still far from
settled struggles over copyright, digital rights management,
file-sharing, plagiarism and piracy on a mass scale.

The constellation of small independent traders selling
creative services and 'content' to distributors is often named
metonymically after the district where the market is clustered:
'Hollywood', 'Tin Pan Alley', 'Wardour Street', 'Fleet Street',
'Silicon Valley' and so on. Actually, getting the general public
to believe that there is such a thing as the media industry, say
in the form of 'Hollywood' (a derivative entity, having no real
existence as such), by continuously 'imagining' or 'inventing'
it in the textual form of news, previews, insider gossip, branding and the like, takes a fair amount of corporate, marketing

and government effort, as John Caldwell (2006) has pointed out. With Web 2.0, more people are asking whether creativity itself and also entrepreneurship are well served by filtering consumer demand through such lumbering metaphors, or whether it might be possible to reconfigure the relationship between producer and consumer on more equal terms. In practice, that means reinventing the market, which is going on now.

## From Industry to (Social Network) Markets

Despite the ill-fitting metaphors, the commonsensical idea of 'industry' suited mass-circulation press and broadcasting well enough, because it was easy to imagine mass communication itself by using yet another metaphor, one that united abstract ideas like 'communication' and 'industry' with a real thing like wire. Thus, industrial production and communication have both been imagined as one-way, with meanings and 'content' proceeding along the value chain as signals do along a cable, as in Claude Shannon's foundational model (1948: 2), which served the field for fifty years:

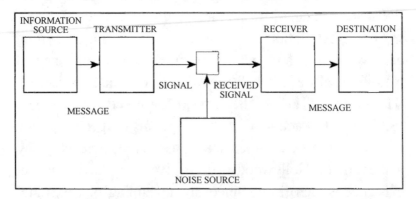

Shannon's 'schematic diagram of a general communication system': one-way mass communication meets the industry value chain

However, the rise of interactive technologies during the Clinton presidency, and the extensive sharing of self-made media thereafter, meant that we could see how contemporary technologies and media might be used for two-way and peer-to-peer social network communication. Instead of an industry doing things to people, here was a market where things are done *by* people. Instead of being represented by the media, or being subjected to the media's own representations, people could self-represent. Transmission went both ways. Popular audiences began to revert from their 'industrial' or passive status as the 'objects' of mass communication to their original 'communicative' status as its agent. They were the source not the destination of mediated meanings (Hartley 2008b).

To account for this, an alternative model of communications was already to hand. The idea of the distributed network was independently developed by the Anglo-Welsh computer pioneer Donald Davies, who came up with the term 'packet switching',[5] and the Polish-American electrical engineer Paul Baran (1964), leading to the earliest visualisation of the internet (Barabasi 2002: 143-5).

We can extrapolate from Baran's model to combine the peer-to-peer attributes of C with the multi-linked hubs of B, resulting in a model of a coordinated social network, one that contrasts starkly with A, a command system based on centralised control. Note that in centralised communication only *control* is extended with each new link. In distributed communication it is the *network* that is infinitely extensible. To achieve a coordinated network, centralised control must in fact be abandoned; complex interconnections emerge into order spontaneously, without a command centre.

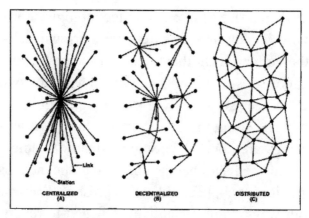

A = control B = coordination C = network

Paul Baran's model of a distributed communication network (the model of the internet). Note that the overlay of B and C forms the model of the social network market - spontaneously coordinated networks with hubs and nodes.

The change in perspective from Shannon to Baran was important. It shifted attention away from model A. This had perhaps unwittingly encouraged a kind of 'colonialist' or 'imperialist' view of industry, where consumers are atomised 'subjects' or effects of causes located elsewhere, 'always already' (in the paranoid lingo; Althusser 2001: 119) positioned in a structure where they have no generative capability of their own; they were effects of power. Instead of this, in a coordinated market (model B + C), consumers could be imagined as being able to 'make a deal' - to agree on an exchange that may also require a continuing relationship - based on some level of calculation of advantage to themselves, as well as paying money or attention to the provider. It's a two-way transaction (dialogue) in a complex network of choices (meaning system).[6]

During the industrial era, profit was generated by investment in the means of production (the Fordist/Taylorite factory system). Even in this period the media were not standard 'industries', because the locus of power and profit in the 'culture industries' was not production but distribution (Garnham 1987). Since the dispersal of massive computing power into the consumer environment (from the 1990s), however, distribution itself has transformed. Even though the TV and media giants are still active, and audiences still watch much more TV than they make for themselves, the 'broadcasting model' of one-way communication, *from a* powerful central agency to dispersed and mutually disconnected passive consumers, is giving way at unprecedented pace to a 'broadband model'. Here consumers are linked in social networks, and productive energy can come from anywhere in the system. Thus, what *Time* called 'a story about community and collaboration on a scale never seen before' - the story of 'you' - is modelling new forms of polity, citizenship and participation for the economic/cultural system as a whole.

## The 'Creative Industries' Concept

Whether user-created content is critiqued as a corporate ruse or celebrated as an opportunity for 'digital democracy' - whether you see a glass as half-empty or half-full - the fact remains that the rise of self-made media poses important questions for 'media industry studies'. A rethink of the metaphor of 'industry' is in order, to include all the agents involved in the system, not just inherited corporate structures. It is also time to abandon the assumption that causation and communication flow one-way only, and to take seriously the agency of the critical-creative citizen-consumer within an overall system in which major enterprises are also at work.

The place where this rethink seems to have progressed

most energetically in recent years is in the new field of 'creative industries' (Hartley (ed.) 2005). The issues raised in the attempt to identify and explain the creative industries are of significance to 'media industry studies', because the creative industries are located at the very place where new values, both economic and cultural, new knowledge and new forms of social relationship are emergent, and where they are in the process of society-wide adoption and retention, often through market mechanisms. It can even be argued that the 'creative industries' are the empirical form taken by innovation in advanced knowledge-based economies, in which case their importance - like that of the media - exceeds their scale as a sector of the economy. It extends to their role as a general *enabling social technology*. This would place *creative innovation* on a par with other enabling social technologies like the law, science and markets. Where the media (in the guise of 'cultural industries') were regarded as the social technology of ideological control in the modern industrial era, the creative industries may be regarded as the social technology of distributed innovation in the era of knowledge-based complex systems. In each case, their value was far greater than their scale as an 'industry sector'. Just as it is not common to assess the importance of the law or of science by counting the number of employees in these occupations, so it is unwise to confine analysis of the media and creative industries to their segment of the overall economic pie-chart. Enabling social (as opposed to physical) technologies provide the framework for the growth of knowledge in general; media and creative innovation play a key role in this process.

However, such a role for creativity was not clear from the outset. The idea of the 'creative industries' had to evolve in practice. Moreover, it seems to be evolving 'sideways' as well as through time; it replicates across several different domains, for instance the arts, the media, and information systems. Successive phases have generated a characteristic economic model and policy response in each domain (Cunningham, Banks & Potts 2008; Potts & Cunningham 2008; Hartley (ed.) 2005):

The 'creative economy': co-present concepts and models of creative industries

| Creative form | Art, individual | Media, industry | Knowledge, market/culture |
|---|---|---|---|
| Model of culture (Williams) | Residual | Dominant | Emergent |
| Economic model | (1) Negative | (2) Neutral | (3) Positive (4) Emergent |
| Policy response | (1) Welfare | (2) Competition | (3) Growth (4) Innovation |

Unlike biological evolution, but like the evolution of culture (Lotman 1990), earlier forms do not suffer extinction. They are supplemented, not supplanted, by their successors. Their co-presence can be ordered dynamically, along the lines proposed by Raymond Williams (1973) for culture itself, which he saw both as 'ordinary' (population-wide, not 'high culture') and as 'a whole way of life' (a system, not a value). His dynamic schema was: residual, dominant, and emergent culture. Thus:

- **Creative industries as art** - generates a 'negative' economic model. Here creativity is seen as a domain of market failure. Art requires subsidy from the rest of the economy. The policy response is therefore a 'welfare' model. This corresponds to a 'residual' dynamic of culture.

- **Creative industries as media industry** - generates a 'neutral' economic model. Media and industries require no special policy attention other than 'competition' policy. This corresponds to 'dominant' culture.
- **Creative industries as knowledge (market and culture)** - generates a 'positive' or an 'emergent' economic model. Here the creative industries are indeed a special case, because they can be seen as the locus for evolutionary growth at the fuzzy boundary between (cultural) social networks and (economic) enterprise, where markets play a crucial role in coordinating the adoption and retention of novelty as knowledge. They require 'growth' and 'innovation' policy. This corresponds to 'emergent' culture (Potts & Cunningham 2008).

The 'positive' (3) or 'emergent' (4) models of a creative economy have only recently been identified and theorised, and are not yet properly 'crunched' in terms of statistical testing. Thus the 'growth' and 'innovation' policy responses themselves remain for the time being an emergent approach to the place and significance of creative innovation in a social totality characterised by growth, dynamism, change and technologically enabled networks on a global scale. If this approach is on the right track, however, it shows that the very term 'industry' is bound to a rapidly obsolescing paradigm, which is associated with a particular economic model and policy response, neither of which is appropriate for current circumstances.

Here, instead of 'industry', a better term is 'market', in

which agents with considerable freedom of choice or flexibility of action make a deal in which something is exchanged (money, attention, connectivity, ideas) for mutual benefit.

After a long, slow build-up, going back to the Enlightenment (Hartley (ed.) 2005: chapter 1), the 'creative industries' burst upon the scene in the 1990s. Since then they have evolved much faster, going through three distinct phases. Each phase shows how a different cultural/economic form is thought to add value in a different way, with a different conceptualisation of the agents of change and dynamism in the system. The concept of creative industries co-evolved with the practice, so the refinement of the model has been as much lived as theorised: it is the product of experience and benefits from the feedback effects of learning.

**The 'creative industries': successive phases (may be co-present)**

| Phase | Form (see previous table) | Value-add | Innovation/ change agent |
|---|---|---|---|
| Enlightenment/ Modernism | Art/reason | Individual talent | Civic humanism |
| Industrialisation | Media | Industry scale | Cultural industries |
| Creative Industries 1 (1995-2005) | Industry | IP outputs | Creative clusters |
| Creative Industries 2 (now) | Market | Creative inputs | Services |
| Creative Industries 3 (emergent) | Knowledge/ culture | Human capital (workforce/user) | Citizen-consumers |

## Industry, Outputs, Clusters

The creative industries were first mapped by the UK government's Department of Culture, Media & Sport (DCMS). In this first phase, attention was focused on the term 'industry' itself, referring to firms whose *outputs* could be construed as creative:

> The creative industries are those industries that are based on individual creativity, skill and talent. They are also those that have the potential to create wealth and jobs through developing intellectual property. The creative industries include: Advertising, Film and video, Architecture, Music, Art and antiques markets, Performing arts, Computer and video games, Publishing, Crafts, Software, Design, Television and radio, Designer fashion.[7]

There has been continuing disagreement about what should be included. This has arisen from problems of scale (global corporations and sole traders in the same category), coherence (what is the unity of 'product' among different creative industries?), scope (potential arbitrariness about what's included and excluded), economic impact (creativity is dispersed across economic sectors, regions, occupations), and, finally, the tendency to neglect the productive role of consumers, users and non-market agencies. Rather than solving these problems conceptually, however, policymakers plumped for Michael Porter's cluster theory, seeking to identify 'cultural quarters' (Roodhouse 2006; but see Oakley & Knell 2007), especially in de-industrialising cities that were redeveloping from centres of production to centres of consumption (tourism, retail, administration and leisure).

It was also argued that creative industries were growing faster than other sectors, claiming extra dynamism for those associated with digital technologies. UK estimates made them worth £112.5 billion in 2001. Variously defined, the creative industries were said to be nearing 10 per cent of the economy in Britain (2006),[8] and nearly 8 per cent of GDP for the United States.[9] In Britain they contributed more than 4 per cent of export income and provided jobs for over two million people.[10] Estimates put the world market at over $3.04 trillion (2005). By 2020; we are told, this sector will be worth $6.1 trillion.[11]

## Market, Inputs, Services

In the second phase, attention widened from creative outputs to the economy as a whole, in order to identify the extent to which creative *inputs* were adding value to firms not otherwise regarded as creative, especially in the *services* sector, for instance government, health, education, tourism, financial services and so on. Creative disciplines, such as design, performance, production and writing, add value to such services. However, it is hard to isolate and quantify the value added, not least because of the way in which industry-based economic statistics are collected and organised. Recent estimates suggest that one-third of those in creative occupations are 'embedded' in other sectors (Higgs et al. 2008).[12]

## Knowledge-Culture, Human Capital, Citizen-Consumers

The third phase is convergent with the extension of digital media into popular culture. The rise of so-called *user-created content* (OECD 2007) has drawn attention to the extent to which innovation, change and growth is attributable not to firms alone but also to *socially networked consumers,* and to non-market activities or 'scenes' that escape traditional economic categories entirely. This phase challenges the closed industrial system of professional expertise, favouring instead the growth of 'complex open networks' in which creative IP is shared, not controlled.

## Creative Industries: Tested to Destruction?

First-player advantage for DCMS meant that its 'cluster' definition captured the attention of policy-makers around the world (more slowly in the United States). Early adopters included many in the Asia-Pacific region, including Hong Kong, Taiwan, Singapore, Australia, New Zealand, and city governments such as Shanghai and Beijing in Mainland China. They adapted the DCMS template to regional realities. Among the best of these is Desmond Hui's report for Hong Kong (CCPR 2003).

Having captured everyone's attention without being conceptually robust, the 'cluster' model required refinement. A sophisticated attempt was made by NESTA (National Endowment for Science, Technology and the Arts), which rejected the original DCMS definition in order to reinstate the industry metaphor: the creative industries seen as 'industrial sectors rather than as a set of creative activities based on individual talent' (NESTA 2006). The NESTA model 'clustered' the creative industries by the type of activity and organisation characteristic of firms. It did not identify such clusters with specific locations such as London; there is slippage between geographical and functional clusters.

## Refined model of the creative industries

**The NESTA 'industry' model: encircling the clusters**
NESTA [National Endowment for Science Technology & the Arts]
(April 2006), *Creating Growth: How the UK Can Develop World
Class Creative Businesses,* NESTA, London, p. 55.

Although the NESTA approach combines phases 1 and
2 by adding 'service providers', the limitations of the word
'industry' only become clearer. The creative industries remain
firmly in the dominant or 'neutral' economic model for which
'competition' policy is the only real recourse.[13] It is hard to
claim any exceptional status for them beyond their importance
to global cities. Under this definition, they remain an esoteric
niche of enterprises that are unified only by drawing a big
circle around incommensurate but overlapping activities:

- media **content**
- **'experiences'** (content you can walk into, like concerts, galleries, parks)
- **'originals'** (un-scalable arts and crafts)
- creative **services** (inputs to other firms; or facilities for rent).

It is hard to extend that idea to the economy in general. However, the political pressure to generalise from 'creative industries' to 'creative economy' was already apparent. The culture minister, Tessa Jowell, announced in 2005 that:

> Every industry must look to become a creative industry, in the broadest sense of the word . . . The increasing array of new and exciting ways to access creative content clearly demonstrates that industry is responding to the needs and expectations of consumers. But these are not just creative industries issues. They are issues for everyone who has a stake in the future of our knowledge economy.[14]

This remained UK policy after the change to Gordon Brown's government, you might even say in the teeth of their own evidence:

> Today there is growing recognition of the subtle but important linkages between the vitality of the creative core, the creative industries beyond and creativity in the wider economy - although uncovering their exact extent is made very difficult because of a paucity of evidence and data.[15]

## Supply to Demand

Since they stem from the same policy-making environment, a static model of the economy, and a 'residual' definition of art, the DCMS and NESTA approaches conceptualise the economy and artistic creativity alike in terms of the *provider* - even as they evolve from phase 1 ('clusters') to phase 2 ('services'), and even as they recognise 'the evolution of experience-searching, so-called "apex" consumers. . . and co-creation with consumers' (Hutton 2007: 96). Despite this gesture, there is no room for consumers *inside* the model.

**The Work Foundation 'economy' model: 'expressive outputs'**
Will Hutton [& the Work Foundation] (June 2007), *Staying Ahead: The Economic Performance of the UK Creative Industries*, DCMS, London, p. 103.

'Industry' continues to mean the supply side of firms or institutions or artists, with no attention to consumers, users or creative individuals, who are seen as an effect of decisions taken by those further up the supply chain or closer to the 'core', with little causal agency of their own. This provider mentality is supported by the 'residual' model of art (for instance as used by David Throsby for his economics of culture; see Hutton 2007: 96, 109; Throsby 2001). See the provider model below.

**Creative industries: creative economy: creative culture**
From . . . supply-side provider-publisher model - ripple-out effect:

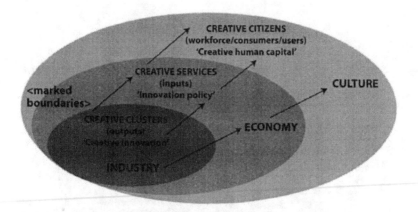

**Provider model of creative causation**

Instead of this, it is now possible to propose a *demand* model of creativity in an evolutionary model of the economy. This sees creative culture in terms of the growth of knowledge among the entire population, not merely among industry or artistic experts. Instead of being the *objects* of causal sequence, consumers, users and citizens become its *subject,* navigating as agents, not being pushed around as passive effects. See the demand model below.

**Agent: network: enterprise**
To ... demand-driven navigator/aggregator - feedback effect:

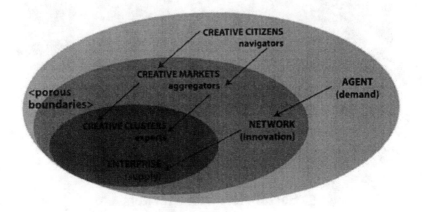

**Demand model of creative causation**

This model pushes out towards the future, not the past; it is an 'emergent' model of innovation. Here creativity may be located as part of 'human capital'. The provider/demand diagrams are of heuristic value only, of course: in reality the arrows always go both ways; see the interactive model on the next page.

**Evolution of knowledge:**

Agents, network and enterprise - interaction process:

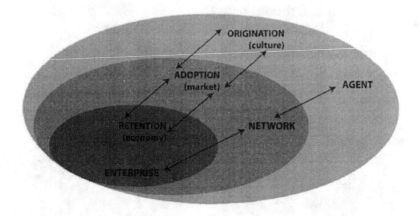

**Interactive model of knowledge growth (open system)**

## Social Network Markets

Seen this way, the evolution of the creative industries does allow us to make a significant conceptual advance, one based on evolutionary economics, and taking seriously the dynamics of change and innovation, the emergence of order in complex systems, and the possibility that both economic and cultural 'behaviour' may be explained using game theory and complexity theory (see Dopfer & Potts 2007; Beinhocker 2006). In this environment, the object of the exercise is to understand the *origination, adoption and retention of knowledge,* not simply to critique the activities of firms. Indeed, focusing on 'industry' has been part of the problem. A better term than 'industry' is 'market', specifically 'social network markets' (Potts et al. 2008). For one thing, it shifts causal sequence from a supply-driven to a demand-driven dynamic. A demand-led model of creative citizen-navigators requires a reformulation of the familiar 'value chain' approach to cultural production, which typically follows a one-way Shannonian logic of causation, like this:

1. **producer** (creation) and production (manufacture)
2. **commodity** (e.g. text, IP) and distribution (via media)
3. **consumer** or audience.

Instead, what is needed is:

1. **agents** *(origination)*, who may be individuals or firms, characterised by choice, decision-making and learning
2. **networks** *(adoption)*, both real (social) and virtual (digital)
3. **enterprise** *(retention)*, market-based organisations and coordinating institutions (Potts et al. 2008).

And instead of linear causation, what is needed is a dynamic and productive interrelationship among *agents, networks* and *enterprise;* all are engaged in the mutual enterprise of creating values, both symbolic and economic. This is a complex open system in which everyone is an active agent, not a closed expert value chain controlled by 'industry'. Individuals originate ideas; networks adopt them; enterprises retain them.

This is the concept of the creative industries as a social network market, the special property of which is that *individual choices are determined by the choices of others within the network.* This is not a difficult concept to grasp; essentially it is Richard Lanham's 'economics of attention' (2006). A social network market is at work whenever you read a review or heed 'word of mouth' before trying a film, restaurant or novelty of any kind. It operates when you value fashion over intrinsic worth. It explains celebrity culture; tastes and identities are formed on the basis of the choices of others. Of course, it underlies 'aggregator' social network enterprises on the internet such as Facebook, MySpace and even YouTube and Amazon, all of which operate by networking individual choices.

Social networks are a valuable adaptive mechanism for dealing with uncertainty, risk and novelty at the macro-scale of populations and systems, even while they are driven by micro-scale individual choices. They occupy the border between established markets (economy) and non-market dynamics (culture), especially via Web 2.0 applications and creative expression. And they work both ways: just as individual consumers decide on this basis what to do, wear, see or even be, so producers respond to the choices of others in deciding where to invest (hence the sequel industry). And neither 'agents' nor 'enterprise' discriminates between producers and consumers, which is of crucial importance in the fast-growing area of user-created content, consumer-led innovation and self-made media. People can make enterprises out of enthusiasms. One moment you're a fan; next you're signing autographs.

## Creative Destruction

Internationally, the essentially European (national public policy; culture) idea of creative industries has collided with the American idea (global free trade; intellectual property). In the process, the 'industrial' concept of the 'consumer' has been complicated by the 'network' idea of the user. Now, computational power and individual consumers can both be theorised as agents of causation and change, and people's 'non-commercial' activities - their culture, knowledge, choices and social networks outside of the economy as such - need to be taken into account, for it transpires that this is where growth, innovation and dynamism originate in the evolution not only of the economy but also of knowledge. Here then is a way to *harness the creative energies of all the agents in the system,* and a mechanism - the social network market - to coordinate their creative and communicative choices and activities on a global scale.

The OECD has reported on the extent of disruptive renewal or 'creative destruction' instigated by consumers in this process:

> User-created content is already an important economic phenomenon despite its originally noncommercial context. The spread of UCC and the amount of attention devoted to it by users appears to be a significant disruptive force for how content is created and consumed and for traditional content suppliers. This disruption creates opportunities and challenges for established market participants and their strategies (OECD 2007: 5).

Indeed, consumers are not only the origin of traditional 'demand' for products and services that established industries are geared up to supply; they also challenge the very business models underpinning those industries:

> New digital content innovations seem to be more based on decentralised creativity, organisational innovation and new value-added models, which favour new entrants, and less on traditional scale advantages and large start-up investments (OECD 2007).

The OECD has listed the socio-cultural 'impacts' of user-created content as follows:

- altered economics of information production
- democratisation of media production

- user autonomy, increased participation and increased diversity
- collaborative, sharing information, ideas, opinions and knowledge
- more diverse array of cultural content
- diversity of opinion, free flow of information and freedom of expression
- challenges - inclusion, cultural fragmentation, content quality and security and privacy; digital divide, cultural fragmentation, individualisation of the cultural environment (OECD: 6).

The impact of user-created content and emergent social network markets on policy has not been fully explored but should not be underestimated. It affects decisions across many areas, including the vexed question of IP law, because a social network market model is much more tolerant of 'piracy' and IP-sharing than is an industry model. Indeed, a country like China may be at a competitive advantage by not having a provider-skewed IP regime. It can get on with promiscuous borrowing and shaping of ideas from wherever they come, just as was the case for the emergent industrial economy in the modernising West. However, as large-scale creative enterprises coalesce in China, the pressure for IP reform will intensify, even though small-scale traders continue to benefit from a 'ducking and weaving' model of regulation. A midway position here may be the Creative Commons movement, associated with Lawrence Lessig, which seeks to find ways to share IP as well as to monetise it (see Leiboff 2007). Beyond the legal framework, the user-created-content/social network market model also affects science and technology policy, industry policy, employment policy and education policy. Doubtless it ought to influence taxation policy too, but that's too hard for me.

## The Growth of Knowledge: A Future for Media Industry Studies?

Looking to the future, it is worth asking whether the recent mass propagation of creative *digital literacy* as part of emergent social network markets may be enabling a further evolutionary step-change in the growth of knowledge. 'Ordinary people' (formerly known as the audience - passive and uneconomic)[16] need to be able to access social network markets as both agents and enterprises, to share their own expertise and to develop new networked expertise ('collective intelligence'), such that they too, as well as professional experts, *contribute to the growth of knowledge.* This ability needs to be propagated via population-wide education (formal and informal) and accounted for in economic modelling. It requires that consumer-created content is seen as more than mere self-expression and communication (leisure entertainment). Digital literacy can generate new forms of 'objective' description and argumentation (Popper 1975), new forms of journalism and new works of the imagination, in which individual consumers are agents in a network, not subjects spiked on the end of advertisers' 'hypodermic' communications. Their individual and collective agency is productive of human knowledge, not simply of corporate takings.

Of course this is already happening, but it is not well integrated into models of mediated communication or policy settings on creative industries, which are still too tied to 'Industry' versus 'Art' (respectively) rather than to integrated knowledge. Instead of ideological stand off, consumer-led innovations need to be understood coherently as emergent knowledge in a complex open system, even while commercialised experiential self-expression - for instance in computer games - looks at first sight like the very opposite of 'knowledge' as we know it (that is, as seen from the perspective of print-based modernity). If pushed beyond an adolescent 'look at me' stage, digital literacy can assist not only in self-expression and communication but also in the development of knowledge in an open innovation network. Consumer-created content is an excellent means for recruiting new participants into that adaptive network, and for lifting general levels of digital literacy and popular expertise. It may be modelling for the coming century the role - if not the methods - of public schooling in the earlier period of print literacy.

The development of social network markets and user-created content should not be seen as an end in itself, then, as if knowledge of the personal is all that is necessary for people outside existing professional elites. It is no advance to reinforce the barriers between popular culture and expert culture: 'science' for producers, 'self' for consumers, or, worse still, 'truth' for the experts and Stephen Colbert's 'truthiness'[17] for the audience. The consequences of doing that are already part of the crisis confronting contemporary societies. People feel cut off from expert systems, including both science and entertainment, and are more sceptical than ever about 'objective knowledge', whether it is presented as science or as news. Not only are the claims and products of scientific research often rejected or delayed in the court of public opinion - CM foods, nuclear energy, WMD, climate change, bioscience - but even the modern commitment to rationality and the open society are undermined from within by resurgent religiosity (including 'new-age' spiritualism), the 'me' culture, and a moralising politics of fear.

The need is not to separate 'science' (description and argumentation) and 'popular culture' (self-expression and communication) further from one another but to invest in holding them together. This is something that creative social networks and social network markets can do, as long as creative digital literacy is propagated on a population-wide basis. The shift from broadcast to interactive media has begun to democratise the publication of self-expression. This is already complicating the entire edifice of 'representation' in both symbolic and political communication, because people can now 'represent' themselves via self-made media. They are no longer satisfied with deferring to professional representatives; they want direct voice, action, creative expression - and, increasingly, knowledge. Creative industries are the generative engine of emergent knowledge.

If the history of print-literacy is anything to go by, democratising digital literacy will unleash presently unthought-of innovations; these may be as remarkable over time as have been the products of print-realism, which include science, the novel and journalism. It is important to include within any account of creative innovation the *emergent* means for growth within the system as a whole. These now include rather than exclude the general public, many of whom are already joining the life of science by contributing directly to the evolution of knowledge. Among the many examples might be Wikipedia (and variants), 'oral' history on the web including digital storytelling and photographic archiving on Flickr, Google Sky (zoom from your house to the universe), SETI (Search for Extraterrestrial Intelligence), computer games for problem-solving, and critical discussion of science versus creationism on YouTube.[18] The 'long tail' means that there are infinitely more examples; what is rarely done in 'critical' media-industry studies is to take these seriously as part of democratised digital media and population-wide social network markets.

The next stage in the evolution of the creative industries is to return the concept to the place where it began - 'creative industriousness', evenly available among the human population, but this time coordinated, scaled and technologically enabled in such a way that social networks can harness the creative imagination of all the agents in the system, which itself can be used for growing knowledge as well as for self-expression. Industry policy, therefore, ought to be directed towards the propagation of digital literacy and participation, and not remain narrowly focused on the firms that service it. If 'human capital' is the most important resource for a creative economy, it follows that education is an important component in the policy mix. However, taking a lesson from the way in which entertainment media do it, education too must be 'demand-led', organised as much through entertainment, media and consumption (use) as through formal schooling. The desire to enjoy creative content within a social network is the mechanism through which learning occurs. These social networks are given life by individual desires, daydreams, mischief-making and play. Self-indulgence by millions of teenagers - extending to whole populations - forms the enabling infrastructure for new knowledge. So a final question on the topic of the future of the media industries is this: what achievements will be enabled by the combination of creative industries, social network markets, mediated entertainment and universal digital literacy? Let's find out.

*'To have great poets, there must be great audiences too.'*
Walt Whitman

# 3

# Bardic Television
## From the 'Bardic Function' to the 'Eisteddfod Function'

### To Have Great Poets ...

Alfred Harbage, pioneering historian of Shakespeare's audience, followed the dictum of the great American poet of democracy Walt Whitman: 'To have great poets, there must be great audiences too' (1883/1995: 324). Harbage (1947) wrote:

> Shakespeare and his audience found each other, in a measure they created each other. He was a quality writer for a quality audience ... The great Shakespearean discovery was that quality extended vertically through the social scale, not horizontally at the upper genteel, economic and academic levels.

I have always been interested in the 'great Shakespearean discovery', which has motivated my research and writing about television ever since *Reading Television* (Fiske &

Hartley 2003 [1978]). In that book, the term 'bardic function' was coined to describe the active relationship between TV and viewers, where, the book argued, TV programming and mode of address use the shared resources of narrative and language to deal with social change and conflict, bringing together the worlds of decision-makers (news), central meaning systems (entertainment) and audiences ('vertically through the social scale') to make sense of the experience of modernity. This chapter revisits the notion of the 'bardic function'. It is an attempt to locate self-made and personally published media, including both community-based initiatives like digital storytelling (see Chapter 5) and commercial enterprises like YouTube, within a much longer historical context of popular narration (see also Chapter 4). The challenge inherent in such an attempt is to understand whether, and if so how, the *cultural function* of the television medium has been affected by recent technologically enabled change. Most important in this respect is the social (and global) dispersal of production. Can TV still serve a 'bardic function' after it has evolved from *broadcast* to *broadband* (and into a further, *mobile* phase)? Broadcast TV has been a household-based 'read-only' medium, with a strong demarcation between highly capitalised expert-professional producers and untutored amateur domestic consumers. Broadband (and mobile) 'TV' is a customised 'read-write' medium, where self-made audiovisual 'content' can be exchanged between all agents in a social network, which may contain any number of nodes ranging in scale from individual, to family-and-friends, to global markets. What continues, and what changes, under such conditions, and what new possibilities are enabled?

## Talk about Full Circle!

Blaming the popular media for immoral, tasteless, sycophantic, sexist, senseless and disreputable behaviour is nothing new. Tut-tutting at the off-duty antics of media personalities also has a long history. Both were present - and already formulaic - at the earliest foundation of European storytelling, in this case sometime before the fourteenth century, and perhaps as far back as the sixth century. This was the period when Taliesin ('Radiant Brow'), Chief Bard of Britain, flourished, or at least when the verses attributed to him were written down. Taliesin 'himself' was both myth and history: a sixth-century historical bard at the court of King Urien of Rheged in North Britain (who too was both historical and a figure in Arthurian myth), and a legendary Taliesin who starred in Welsh poems associated with his name in the *Book of Taliesin* (Guest 1849; Ford 1992).

On the occasion when he first revealed his magical poetic powers, this fictional Taliesin delivered a series of poems denouncing the king's existing corps of four and twenty bards. Part of the trick of getting himself noticed, evidently, was to rubbish the opposition:

**Strolling minstrels** are addicted to evil habits.
**Immoral songs** are their delight.
In **a tasteless manner** they rehearse the praise of heroes.
**Falsehood** at all times they use . . .

*Cler o gam arfer a ymarferant*
*Cathlau aneddfol fydd eu moliant*
*Clod orwas ddiflas a ddatcanant*

*Celwydd bob amser a ymarferant*

| | |
|---|---|
| The **fair virgins** of Mary they corrupt. | *Morwynion gwinion mair a lygrant* |
| Those who put **trust** in them they bring to **shame,** | *A goelio iddynt a gwilyddiant* |
| And **true men** they **laugh** to scorn, | *A gwyrion ddynion a ddyfalant* |
| And **times and seasons** they spend in vanities . . . | *A hoes ai amser yn ofer y treuliant* |
| All kinds of **senseless stories** they relate. | *Pob parabl dibwyll a grybwyllant* |
| All kinds **of mortal sins** they praise. | *Pob pechod manvol a ganmolant* |

Taliesin, *Fustl y Beirdd* ['Flail of the Bards'], Nash (1858), pp. 177-9.[1]

If you substitute 'TV and pop culture' for 'strolling minstrels', and in terms of cultural function there's every reason why you should, then this list of evil, immorality, tastelessness, lies, exploitation of women, abuse of trust, humiliation of innocent citizens, time-wasting vanity and senselessness is surprisingly familiar. It's just the kind of thing that people say about the 'tabloid' media, popular entertainment formats and media celebrities (e.g. see Lumby 1999; Turner 2005). Taliesin's name, which by the time these lines were composed was itself a popular 'brand' or 'channel',[2] was used to reproach the other bards, 'so that not one of them dared to say a word' (Guest 1849), a fatal condition in a bard. Evidently, a *competitive system* of knowledge-providers was already well developed in pre-modern oral culture, in which 'media professionals' vied openly for both institutional patronage and popular acclaim. Later commentators on Taliesin have supposed that the composer of this invective against strolling minstrels - who were the *distribution system* for pre-modern popular media - was likely to have been a thirteenth- or fourteenth-century monk, usurping Taliesin's name for a contemporary dispute. There was no love lost between monks and minstrels. Their mutual loathing was occasioned not only by a difference between sacred/clerical and secular/profane world views but also by a medieval antecedent of the modern antagonism between public-service and commercial media, education and entertainment, high and popular culture, artistry and exploitation, intellectuals and showmen. Proponents of the former have persistently called for official regulation of the latter. And this too is nothing new: by the tenth century it had already occurred in the legal code of Hywel Dda (King Howell the Good), laying down the infrastructure for cultural distinctions that persist to this day.[3]

Generically, the despised but ubiquitous medieval 'popular media' - the romances and narrative verse collected under the name of Taliesin and others and distributed by strolling minstrels - were comparable to the style of variety, magazine and current affairs shows on television. The overall mix in a given performance did not follow the Aristotelian unities of place, time and action, but included successive snippets of news, fantasy, ballad, romance, travel, discovery and morality, all presented in an entertaining package that borrowed freely from other suppliers but made sure that audiences knew which noble sponsor was behind it (by praising same to the skies) and which poetic brand - in this case the top 'brand' of Taliesin - was bringing them these pleasures:

Written down from the mouths of the wandering minstrels ... the poems ascribed to Taliesin in particular, are for the most part made up of allusions to local, sometimes historical events, references to the *Mabinogion,* or fairy and romance tales of the Welsh, scraps of geography and philosophy, phrases of monkish Latin, moral and religious sentiments, proverbs and adages, mixed together in wonderful confusion, sometimes all in the compass of one short ballad (Nash 1858: 34-5).

Welcome to television, Taliesin-style.

## Bardic Television: 'From the Hall of the Baron to the Cabin of the Boor'

When we coined the term 'bardic function', Fiske and I wanted to identify the cultural rather than the individual aspect of television. We did not share the then predominant approaches to audiences, derived as they were from psychology (media effects on individual behaviour), sociology (the 'uses and gratifications' of television) and political economy (consumers as effects of corporate strategies). Such approaches looked for a linear chain from TV (cause) to audiences (effect), as in "TV causes violence'. We approached TV audiences from a cultural perspective and a literary training, which meant:

- seeing television and its audiences as part of an overall **sense-making system,** like language and its elaborated or 'literary' forms and genres, both verbal and visual
- seeing culture not just as a domain of aesthetics but also, and primarily, as one of identity-formation, power and struggle; **the performance of the self in the context of power**
- trying to find a way of connecting the institutionalised **cultural, linguistic** and

**audiovisual** resources of modern culture, especially popular media and entertainment, with the individual talents,
aspirations, inner life and creativity of ordinary people,
on the model of the literate 'reading public' but massively
extended to media audiences.

Within this envelope of meaningfulness a 'whole way of
life' is established, made sense of, lived and changed, render-
ing media consumption as an *anthropological* sense-making
activity (e.g. Richard Hoggart, Raymond Williams, Claude
Levi-Strauss, Marshall Sahlins, Edmund Leach; see Hawkes
1977). Combining the cultural approach with a mode of
analysis derived from *semiotics,* which is interested in how
the overall sense-making system works to generate new
meanings at various levels of symbolism (e.g. Ferdinand
de Saussure, Roland Barthes, Umberto Eco, Yuri Lotman),
we argued that TV brought together in symbolic unity, by
means of specialised textual forms from cop shows to quiz
shows, the worlds of a society's leadership (top) and its
general population (bottom), just as had the Tudor propa-
gandist William Shakespeare. And just as John Milton had
updated from Homer the purpose of epic poetry, seeking
to explain the human condition and to 'justify the ways of
God to men' *(Paradise Lost* 1667: 1.26), so contemporary
media storytelling, updated from poetry to long-form drama
and reality TV, serves to expose the human condition and
to 'justify' (that is, imagine, explain and assess) the 'ways
of power' to audiences (Gibson 2007). In deference to the
literary, historical and anthropological antecedents of our
work, and to television's own oral-musical modes of address, not to mention the contextual fact that at the time

Fiske and I worked in Wales, we called that justification process the 'bardic function'.

The antecedents of popular entertainment with political import go as far back at least as the medieval bards, heralds, minstrels and troubadours whose job it was to 'broadcast' the exploits, ferocity, largesse and (mis)adventures of the high and mighty. In other words, the 'bardic function' retains some ancient aspects, not only those relating to universal human creative talent, but also in organisational form and purpose:

> That bards or persons gifted with some poetic and musical genius existed in Britain, as in every other country in the world at every age, may be conceded, and that among the Celtic tribes, perhaps in an especial manner, the capacity for recording in verse the deeds of warriors and the ancestry of chieftains, was held in high esteem, and the practice an honourable occupation (Nash 1858: 24).

Why is such an occupation honoured? Of what use is it to the polity? For those he served directly, the Celtic bard was of high importance as the broker of knowledge for the family he served (which stood in place of the state at the time). Bardic song brought new information and ideas into the court, while simultaneously broadcasting to the world the employer's claims to fame. The bard was:

> ... the genealogist, the herald, and to some extent the historian of the family to which he was attached, kept alive the warlike spirit of the clan or tribe, the remembrance of the old feuds or alliances, and whiled away those tedious hours of an illiterate age ... To some extent a man of letters, he probably fulfilled the office of instructor in the family of his patron or chief (Nash 1858: 27).

For the remainder of society, a 'mass medium' was needed to broadcast the adventures and to advertise the merits of the winners in the medieval 'economy of attention' (Lanham 2006). Although it had its clerical detractors, as we have seen, such a medium existed in the minstrelsy:

> Besides these regularly acknowledged family or domestic Bards, there was in Wales, in the eleventh and twelfth centuries, and from thence downwards, a very numerous class of itinerant minstrels, who, like the Toubadours, Jongleurs, or Glee-men, wandered from place to place, seeking reward for the entertainment they afforded by their musical acquirements, and their recital of songs and tales for the amusement of all classes, from the hall of the baron to the cabin of the boor (Nash 1858: 27).

*Reading Television* (2003: 64-6) listed seven qualities shared by bards and television. Both are:

1. **mediators** of language
2. expressions **of cultural** needs (rather than formal purity or authorial intention)
3. **socio-central**
4. **oral** (not literate)
5. **positive and dynamic** (their storytelling mode is to **'claw back'** anomalous or exogenous events such that nothing in the external environment remains unintelligible or outside of the frame of bardic textualisation; and everything they publish is intelligible to the general audience)
6. myth-making
7. sources and repositories **of common sense and conventions** of seeing and knowing.

The *function* of the 'bardic function' is to textualise the world meaningfully for a given language community. Goran Sonesson has put this diagrammatically:

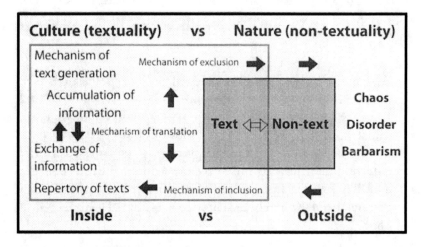

**'Tartu school' semiotic model of culture**
Goran Sonesson (1997), 'The limits of nature and culture in cultural semiotics', in Richard Hirsch (ed.), *Papers from the Fourth Bi-annual Meeting of the Swedish Society for Semiotic Studies,* Linkoping University, December; and (2002), 'The culture of Modernism: From transgressions of art to arts of transgression', in M. Carani & G. Sonesson (eds), *Visio,* 3, 3: *Modernism,* pp. 9-26.

*Reading Television* (2003: 66-7) enumerated the functions performed by TV in its bardic role:

- to articulate cultural consensus
- to implicate individuals in the cultural value-system
- to celebrate the doings of cultural representatives
- to affirm the practical utility of myths and ideologies in the context of conflict (both real and symbolic)
- to expose, conversely, perceived inadequacies in the cultural sense of self

- to convince audiences that their status and identity as individuals is guaranteed
- to transmit a sense of cultural membership.

By this analogy - although I am trying to show that this is more than an analogy; it was an evolutionary build-up of cultural and organisational resources - the 'bardic function' of popular television works to 'sing the praises' of its dominant culture in the same way that Celtic bards and minstrels lauded, lamented and sometimes laughed at their overlords in an oral culture, sharing amusement and adventure among all classes 'from the hall of the baron to the cabin of the boor'. Both bard and box connect political power and textual pleasure in a specialised form of expression that is accessible to everyone in a given language community, and which serves the function of ordering the social, natural and supernatural worlds. Although bardic tales were *about* knights and princesses, they were *for* everyone - as they remain, in fantasy genres. A good example can be seen in Brian Helgeland's 2001 movie A *Knight's Tale* (starring the late Heath Ledger), whose character 'Chaucer' (Paul Bettany) imaginatively re-creates the 'bardic function' with poetic verve if not complete historical verisimilitude. Like Taliesin in Celtic Britain, television uses high-level narrative conventions and its own oral/aural (rather than literate) relationship with audiences to spin topical but timeless stories out of the doings of contemporary characters, many of these the latter-day equivalent of the kings, beasts and heroes of the Middle Ages (Jones 1972), albeit in the convincing guise of detectives, prostitutes, journalists, celebrities, neighbours or foreigners.

## Narrative and Polity - 'Representation of the People'

It should be noted that the order of bards and popular television alike are specialised institutional agencies for delivering the 'bardic' function in a given culture. They take it on and professionalise it within evolving historical, regulatory and economic contexts, and of course in so doing they tend to narrow its potential, to exclude outsiders (the general public) from productive or creative participation, not least to maintain the price of their skills, and to restrict the infinite potential of semiosis to definite forms with which their own institutionalised 'mechanism of translation' (see figure on page 80) can comfortably cope. These institutional agencies can optimise storytelling's scale (a story can be reproduced many times) and its diffusion (a story can be heard by many people); but they also increase both formal and bureaucratic rigidity ('transaction costs') in narrative production and thus reduce adaptability to change.

Such a view of the 'bardic function' must retain a 'top-down' approach to storytelling, because it focuses on a centralised 'institutional' form of production, rather than storytelling at the 'anthropological' level of everyday life. Bardic tales were about the elite who commissioned the bards to tell them. They were made by specialist professionals close to the centres of power. They were intended for the enjoyment of one and all, and designed to be diffused throughout the social strata and across the land or indeed the world, as in the global career of Arthurian stories. Broadcast television certainly cast the semiotic net more widely, telling tales of ordinary life using characters from across the social spectrum (a vernacular innovation pioneered in Chaucer's *Canterbury Tales)*. However, in neither the bardic nor the broadcast context did 'ordinary' people play much of a direct role in the production of these tales. During the heyday of television, the domestic TV audience could participate only by gathering round and enjoying official versions performed by professional bards and minstrels. They were not encouraged to take up the metaphorical harp for themselves and have a go too, using the shared forms and conventions of the style.

The concept of the 'bardic function' was developed specifically to account for the storytelling mode of a mass medium, in which a few storytellers 'sang' universally accessible narratives about socially favoured characters to many auditors, and thereby gave shape, and sometimes purpose, to the polity as a whole. A limitation of this top-down perspective, as Llewelyn Wyn Griffith pointed out in relation to the period of the medieval princes immortalised in bardic song, is that 'we do not know what the common man [much less woman or child] thought of it all' (Griffith 1950: 80). Neither their own words nor the stories of their lives are preserved in text, which at this stretch of time is the only archive remaining to tell us something about the culture. The same might be said of mass media, which tend to tell stories of ordinary life to 'the common man' and woman and child, in the form of comedy, soap opera and reality television, but nevertheless, simply for reasons of scale, cannot accommodate more than samples of expression *by* them.

But now, everyone with access to a computer can not only 'sing' for themselves, they can also personally publish the results to everyone else. The shift from the broadcast to the interactive era, from analogue to digital technologies, and from expert/professional production to DIY or 'consumer-generated' content - from 'read only' to 'read and write' media, for consumers as well as professionals - has opened up the idea of the 'bardic function' to new interpretation, and to a new challenge. A new *interpretation* must include this widely distributed capability, with myriad storytellers not just top bards.

How far into 'ordinary' life might the production and performance of stories go? In terms of oral cultures like those of pre-modern Europe, such an interpretation would require attention not just to 'court' bards but also to 'folk' songs and stories, from art to anthropology, from the productivity of a social institution to that of language. A new interpretation of the 'bardic function' would need to take a much stronger interest in what has come to be called 'amateur', DIY or consumer-created content. The *challenge* is to understand how such a diffused system might work to propagate coherent sense across social boundaries, among different demographics and throughout social hierarchies. In other words, how does a fully distributed narrative system retain overall systemic unity? If everyone is speaking for themselves, then who speaks for everybody?

This is a similar question to one of the central problems of democracy itself, which is always beset by secessionist tendencies (see Collier & Hoeffler 2002), and only seems to work at any scale once it has abandoned direct decision-making in favour of some form of representative delegation, so that the demos is included symbolically rather than literally in the decision-making process of the polity. As with democracy, so with musical or dramatic storytelling - the challenge is to find a way to think about, to explain and to promote mass participation without encouraging splits, divisions, migrations and anarchy on the one hand, or an incomprehensible cacophonous plurality of competing voices on the other, or an authoritarian/elitist alternative to both. The challenge is also a negative one - how *not* to associate 'more' with 'worse'; mass participation with loss of quality.

Can one imagine a 'bardic function' that pervades the polity, that keeps open the possibility of communication and meaningfulness across demographic boundaries and social hierarchies, providing leadership as to what 'we' know and imagine, while simultaneously permitting everyone's unique experiences to be connected to (and differentiated from) common knowledge and popular entertainment? And can one imagine stories told by *just anyone* as simultaneously democratic in expression yet retaining the admired qualities of professionally crafted work?

Such an extended function is like *language* itself rather than being the direct product or purpose of a state or other institutional 'provider'. A language unites the unpredictable unique utterances produced by all speakers with the systematic coherence required for them to be heard, understood and responded to by any hearer within the given language community. Nevertheless, language too has been subjected to institutional organisation, official regulation and historical evolution; and it has developed complexity in both form and content. In medieval courts, language was institutionally differentiated from action, bards from knights, *prating* from *prowess*. Each function was separately organised into its own 'order' with its own regulations, rituals and specialist schools. Bards were servants of the king (or state), from which position - like media barons - the successful ones achieved influence, status and wealth. However, in one sense, and in the long run, they were even more powerful than kings. For they were the creators of a kind of cultural wealth that was and remains in short supply and great demand - immortality through fame. Kings and knights were not known until praised. So of course they all did whatever it took, in a competitive system, to make sure that their actions were noted and remembered (including paying for that service). The 'age of chivalry' was a product of those who recorded it, not directly of the knights whose actions were celebrated. In the long run you were only as brave or successful as Taliesin (et al.) said you were; the memory of your very existence depended upon story. This was the origin of both literature and heraldry. Bards, minstrels and heralds performed the same job, that of noting exactly who was who, what they did to deserve their honour, and which family or court should get the credit (College of Arms n.d.).

Fame followed flattery - not the other way around. Unlauded, the common people were not known at all. A full scale 'economy of attention' (Lanham 2006) was in place, comprising a competitive social network market in which everyone's value was determined by what everyone else in the system knew and said about them (Potts et al. 2008). This was a 'virtualisation' or 'textualisation' of what had since very ancient times been a literal and material practice. The Achaeans, for instance, measured honour directly, in booty won in battle. It was called *geras*. After a battle the 'spoils of war' (captured arms, people, towns and so on) were literally divided up among the winning warriors by the victorious general or king; and the bigger your pile the more you were honoured. Conversely a small pile was an insult, so further conflict or defection was likely over the 'distributive fairness' of the division of spoils (Balot 2001: 87-8).[4] But of course we only know all this because a poet - in this case Homer - duly noted it down, recording both the system of *geras* and the amount apportioned to Achilles, Ajax, Hector and others, by which 'honours' the immortality of these heroes is still measured today.

## 'Olympic Games of the Mind'

For humans, storytelling itself is a form of schooling in the capabilities of language. It teaches us how to think (plot), what to think about (narrative), the moral universe of choice (character) and the calculation of risk (action), motivated by desire for immortality (fear of death). If learning via storytelling is so important, you might expect to find it institutionalised, brought out from the realm of tacit or informal knowledge into the scientific realm of explicit expertise. For even if it is the case that storytelling is, as it were, an evolutionary adaptation, it does not follow that natural talent will thrive naturally. As well as any natural propensity among individuals, its propagation requires social coordination to extend it throughout the population via progressive stages of tutelage to attain higher levels of complexity, and 'the oxygen of publicity' to make it all seem worth attempting. Thus, even though everyone can tell a story, storytelling needs infrastructural investment if it is to answer the needs of an increasingly adept population in a growth-economy. If stories are teachers, how can storytelling be taught? Are there social institutions devoted to propagating the skill among the many, rather than restricting its benefits to the few?

Historically, part at least of the answer to that question

was bardic. Bardic schools were instituted in medieval times in Wales and Ireland to systematise the order of bards and to teach subjects we might now recognise as law, history, geography, genealogy, language, literature, music, science (e.g. natural history, magic) and religion, as well as - indeed through - the strict regulations appertaining to bardic poetry in terms of form, metre (cynghanedd, englynion) and so on.[5] Such schools were far from informal, but they were oral and vernacular in mode, unlike ecclesiastical schools (from which modern schooling is descended), which were literate and Latinate. Bardic schools precipitated into the general population people who were skilled in the craft aspects of storytelling as well as knowledgeable in the topical issues, powers and celebrities of the day.

One of the earliest social mechanisms used to improve bardic quality was the *eisteddfod* (literally 'sitting'). The first eisteddfod was held (it is said) in the court of Rhys ap Gruffudd, prince of Deheubarth in South Wales, in 1176.[6] This 'grand festival' was an open, international competition, announced a year in advance, to find the best bard and the best minstrel. Competitors congregated at Lord Rhys's place, Cardigan (Cadwgan) Castle, and each was given hospitality and the two winners received 'vast gifts'. These professional eisteddfodau continued periodically until the decline of the bardic order by the seventeenth century. They were revived by Iolo Morgannwg (Edward Williams), 'a stonemason of ill-controlled genius' (Griffith 1950: 143), on Primrose Hill in London in 1791, as a vehicle for the expression of passionate amateurism and (largely fabricated) antiquarianism.

**A Prince of Wales visits Cardigan Castle, more than 800 years after the first eisteddfod was held there by an earlier Prince of Wales**
Photograph courtesy of the *Tivyside Advertiser* and Cadwgan/Cardigan Castle.

From 1860 the National Eisteddfod was held each summer. It continues today as one of the main cultural events of Wales. It is held entirely in Welsh, to determine and showcase the winners of bardic, musical and literary competitions, among others - there are sections for science and media too. A popular annual holiday event, it attracts an average of over 150,000 visitors each year, from a population of three million of whom about one-fifth are Welsh-speakers (Stevens & Associates 2003: 11-16). A cross between folk festival (e.g. Glastonbury in Britain, Woodford in Australia, the National in the United States), scholarly convention[7] and *Pop Idol,* the National Eisteddfod has remained a national but amateur institution of language and learning for many decades.

Writing of this 'one-nation Olympic games of the mind',
Llewelyn Wyn Griffith (1950) asked: 'Where else can you
find a people eager to devote a week to crowding into a
peripatetic festival devoted to the arts, ordinary people,
working people, men and women of all ranks, rich and
poor?' (152). Despite his conviction that 'there is nothing
quite like it anywhere else in the world' (136), there are in
fact quite a few things like it. Carnivalesque singing and
poetry competitions abound, in folk, urban and school settings. Some of them are modelled on and retain the title of
the 'eisteddfod', including well-established networks in
former imperial dominions like Australia and South Africa.[8]
Some don't use the Welsh word, but eisteddfodau they are;
for example:

> . . . several hundred people ascended to the Waswantu Plateau
> in the southern Peruvian Andes to celebrate and compete in an
> annual song contest that marks the height of carnival festivities
> in the region . . . Competing groups regaled the assembled crowd
> and judges throughout the day with newly composed songs that
> ranged, in usual carnival fashion, from the bawdy to the biting,
> the raunchy to the reflective (Ritter 2007: 177).

These events maintain a strongly local and self-made character. They are not swamped by global media and power; rather
they are an exercise in rereading it. The Andean event described
above attracted the attention of ethnomusicologist Jonathan
Ritter because, 'late in the day . . . the "Falcons of Mt Wam-
aqo" entered the ring of rocks marking the performance area
and offered its final-round entry, a song entitled "Osama bin
Laden".' As Emma Baulch has commented, writing about the
punk music scene in Bali: 'due to the global dissemination

of mass mediation, people now collectively imagine exis-
tences that differ from the social realities in which they live.
Thus the electronic media's impact on the imagination serves
not just as an escape but as a staging ground for action' (Baulch
2007: 110-11). Globally dispersed competitive performance
carnivals like eisteddfodau (under whatever local name) are
among the training camps for that staging ground. They have
appropriated contemporary media, as well as using oral traditions and professional skills going back a thousand years and
more. They are used for the present purposes of non-elite populations, brought together in a 'great feast of amateurs of the arts'
(Griffith 1950: 147), one in which a people self-organises to
propagate and improve its own use of its own language.

A connection between the amateur eisteddfod and the
expert media remains, because the competitions held in
schools and community centres and on mountainsides are
used by performers, parents and professional associations
alike as an apprenticeship training ground - a 'beauty pageant
circuit', as it were, for voices, words and music. Out of it
can certainly come world-class talent, as demonstrated in the
life and career of opera star Bryn Terfel, who was raised on
eisteddfodau and now produces and sponsors them.[9] And of
course mainstream or traditional media have developed their
own highly coded versions of the eisteddfod, in the guise of
the *'Idol'* format - which, it transpires, goes back to Prince
Rhys ap Gruffudd's contest, the *Bardic Idol* of the 1170s.

## 'Bamboo Shoots after the Rain' - Proliferating Global Eisteddfodau

The Rock Eisteddfod is a hybrid form that has had success in
Australia, and thence in Japan, New Zealand, South Africa,

Germany, Dubai and the United Kingdom. It is a national competitive event for schools, designed to 'motivate young Australians to make positive and healthy lifestyle choices'.[10] The idea is to combine music, performance and health messages. Originally promoted by a radio station, the finals are now televised, and successful school teams may tour overseas. The 'challenge' targets youth at risk of 'abuse, discrimination, crime or drugs, neglect or destructive behaviour'. In 2008 the Rock Eisteddfod 'Global Challenge' was held in Japan, where performances were to be staged using a contemporary remix of traditional Japanese tales.[11] Advice to contestants on the website included a presentation on 'Creating a Theme', which gave examples of how to find, research and remix a story. The similarity between these Japanese stories and those to be found under Taliesin's name in the *Mabinogion* is striking - and highly appropriate to a global eisteddfod.

Here are some extracts from the Japan Rock Challenge's 'Creating a Theme':

Japanese folklore themes:

- *mukashibanashi* - tales of long-ago
- *ongaeshibanashi* - stories of repaying kindness
- *tonchibanashi* - witty stories
- *waraibanashi* - funny stories
- *yokubaribanashi* - stories of greed
- *namidabanashi* - sad stories
- *obakebanashi* - ghost stories.

Examples of stories:

- Kintaro, the superhuman Golden Boy
- the vengeful Kiyohime, who became a dragon

- Momotaro, the om-slaying Peach Boy
- Bancho Sarayashiki, the ghost story of Okiku and the Nine Plate
- Urashima Taro who rescued a turtle and visited the bottom of the sea
- Yotsuya Kaidan, the ghost story of Oiwa
- Issun-Boshi, the One-inch Boy
- Kachi Kachi Yama, a villainous raccoon-dog and heroic rabbit
- Bunbuku Chagama, a teakettle which is actually a shape-changing *tanuki*
- Hanasaka Jiisan, the old man that made the flowers bloom
- Tamamo no Mae, the wicked fox-woman
- Shira-kiri Suzume, the tongue-cut sparrow.

One possibility is to remix the oldest story of them all:

*Taketori Monogatari (The Tale of the Bamboo Cutter)* written in the 10th century is the oldest surviving Japanese work of fiction. It is often referred to as the 'ancestor of all romances'. Theories as to the background of the story have never been proven, e.g. the names of five suitors are those of members of the Japanese court in the 8th century that the story is directed at etc. Today it is known as a children's story, *Kaguya-hime (Princess Kaguya),* and shares similarities with *Sailor Moon, Cinderella, Thumbeiina, Snow White* and even *Rocket Girls* anime.

Students were advised that in remixing such a story the purpose was to 'carry a message':

The Japanese proverb - **'Ugo no takenoko'** - translates as **'bamboo shoots after the rain'**. This expression suggests that, as in life, many things happen one-after-another, just as bamboo shoots bursting to the surface after the rain. And it is how we react and respond to difficult or seemingly impossible situations that defines who we are. This becomes the performance 'challenge'... to explain in music, drama and dance this 'message' to the audience: that life is ... MISSION: POSSIBLE.[12]

## Digital Literacy - From Self-Made Media to Self-Made Networks

The unusual thing about digital storytelling compared with other digital products is that it is taught. It has about it more of the eisteddfod than the software application. It prioritises the 'storytelling' over the 'digital' - indeed it is pretty hard to find on the net. Instead, digital storytelling thrives among the very same community centres, voluntary organisations and arts activists who devote their time to improving the creative and performative talents of the otherwise untutored multitude, encouraging those with tradable talent to move into professional levels of the system (cultural or economic), while enabling those who otherwise only get to stand and stare to tell their own stories. In short, the propagation of digital storytelling is more like the teaching of music than like the marketing of media. Digital storytelling is a 'practice' rather than a 'form'; a story *circle* that links tellers with other agents across the network. On the model of other institutions of vernacular teaching like the eisteddfod, it shows how entire institutional *networks* as well as individual *stories* can be 'self-made'.

This is how the eisteddfod reconfigures the 'bardic function'. The oral bardic function of storytelling *for* a culture is an evolutionary antecedent to a networked bardic function of storytelling *by a* culture. As a result, 'self-actualisation' can now be an individual activity rather than a representative story - something we do, not something we watch. However, even individual talent needs development, and various vernacular institutions, including eisteddfodau, have arisen to service that need. People are not encountered as single selves even when they are telling their own story. Instead, through informal institutions that help the system as a whole to coordinate and replicate its capabilities, individuals are encountered as connected and networked interlocutors, able to speak for themselves but only because they are in a context where conversation is possible with others and others are present to add their own voices.

This being the case, a question remains about the role of professional 'bards'. The original bards were the highest exponents of the literacy of the time: they expressed the possibilities afforded by the textual system of oral poetry; they were the innovators, the sources of growth; in short, they were the semiotic wealth-creators of their day and they were royally rewarded for it. From that perspective, handing over the baton to the amateur audience may seem like a backward step, a lowering of standards, and a threat to income (see Chapter 5). The idea that each individual should tell his or her own story may even encourage self-regarding 'look-at-me' egotism among the 'reading public'. Now, it seems, we don't have to earn attention, esteem or honour or have it bestowed by a specialist, as in the days of heralds and bards, because we can just say whatever we like about ourselves on Bebo. All citizens become their own Homer, their own Taliesin, blowing their own heraldic trumpet, 'harping on' in bardic style, singing their own praises. Some 'experts' regard such a prospect not as democratised expression or consumer productivity but as a nightmare scenario (Keen 2007).

However, things are clearly not as simple as this. To tell their own stories people must be able not only to record something that happened and how they feel about it but also how it might sound to an interlocutor, what there is about it that might attract an audience's attention, and what it might tell people that they don't already know. In other words, people must learn not only the basic skills of *self-expression* but also those of effective *communication;* not only to tell stories but also to attend to their hearers' demands for information, education and entertainment (as the BBC mantra had it). In an open system they will also learn how to connect what they want to say with what others in the network are saying and want to hear.

In this way, people are now able to toggle between the 'oral' romanticism of self-presence and dialogue on the one hand and the 'literate' realism of abstract ideas and anonymous dissemination on the other. Indeed, blogging theorist Jill Walker Rettberg (2008) claims that it is exactly this combination of personal *dialogue* and public *dissemination* that marks the blog as an advance beyond both oral and literate media of communication: 'they allow more dialogue than the pre-digital written word, and allow even cheaper and more extensive distribution than print or broadcasting' (56). Furthermore, everyone can play, as both individual and as 'the general public': 'Today, new kinds of literacy are developing as the general population is acquiring new skills and the ability to read and navigate the Web and to publish its own words, images, videos, blogs and other content' (39).

By improving such literacies, the standard of individual utterance and of the entire social network is cumulatively raised. Thence the most interesting question is what digital media might be used *for.* We should wait and see, not fall for the temptation of hurling abuse at the latest upstart medium that poses some sort of competition to the entrenched professionals of the day, just as the mythical Taliesin did in his own diatribe against the strolling minstrels. It is an unedifying sight, serving only to mask the real potential of the contemporary 'bardic function'. Instead, it would be preferable to show how the massive scaling-up of storytelling expands rather than supersedes the opportunities for professional storytellers and 'ordinary' people alike - consumer productivity and trained expertise are both required if the energies of all agents in the system are to be harnessed.

In such a context, professional storytellers have options:

- **The Taliesin function** ('I'm a bard and you're not'). They can carry on doing what they do so well, and thumbing their noses at the 'amateurs', for as long as the 'top-down' business plan allows it.
- **The Gandalf function** ('I'm a bard and this is how it's done'). They can shift, as educators have learnt to do, from the position of 'sage on the stage' to that of 'guide on the side' or even 'meddler in the middle' (McWilliam 2007). In other words, they can use their skills to assist the productivity of the storytelling system rather than seeking to dominate it, helping to make the intuitive skills of others explicit and goal-directed, rather than usurping them.

- **The eisteddfod function** ('We're all bards: let's rock!'). This third option beckons. It takes up the baton of the eisteddfod, proposing amateur and professional as options within the same system, not as opposed paradigms, thereby leading to the possibility of co-creative collaboration that massively extends the capability of the system.

As time elapses, things evolve. Based on the lesson of previous step changes in the growth of knowledge, it is clear that evolution is blind, and the opportunities afforded by adaptations cannot be known in advance, whether it is the opposable thumb or the digital network. Certainly, when writing and printing were invented, no-one could have predicted their eventual uses from the purposes of the inventors. The printing press in Gutenberg's day was based on agricultural machinery and used largely for religious clients. Its eventual success was not at all certain. Like many innovative start-ups, Gutenberg's own firm went bust and was bought out by his financial investor and his assistant. It was not Gutenberg but Fust & Schöffer who were responsible for the exploitation of printing; Gutenberg himself made not a brass razoo out of it (Presser 1972: 354). Fust & Schöffer marketised Gutenberg's technological invention; and, although few will have heard of them now, it was their success that ensured the adoption and retention of printing as an evolutionary success and not just another experimental 'mutation'.

Even after it was well established, no-one could have foreseen the importance of printing and publishing for the growth of the great realist textual systems of modernity - science, journalism and the novel - since none of them existed until printing made possible the development of a modern reading public. Similarly, who today can predict the cultural function of internet affordances, the outcome of the democratisation of publishing, and the population-wide extension of semiotic productivity? Here is where creative professionals might focus their attention, by seeing the bardic function as socially distributed and evolutionary, while seeking to maximise its current potential for self-expression, social networking and knowledge-creation. What can the system make possible now that it has been invented?

We don't yet know the answer to that question. It's an emergent system. In the meantime, it is sufficient perhaps to focus on what individuals have to say, especially by adding to the social conversation as many as possible of the voices belonging to the 'common man and woman' who have historically left so little trace on explicit knowledge or elaborated language. This is what self-made and self-published online media allow for. They show how literacy belongs to the system, not to individuals, that the system requires both individual agents (bards) and organising institutions (the eisteddfod), and that professionalism, innovation, novelty, creativity and knowledge are, in principle, universally distributed among agents who can navigate their own way to their own objectives, creating knowledge as they go; and 'performing the self, in the context not only of power but also of possibility. It remains true now as it was in Walt Whitman's day that 'to have great poets, there must be great audiences too'. The 'eisteddfod function' of latter-day competitive individualism in socially networked creative systems is one excellent but under-appreciated way of nurturing great audiences.

*'Those who tell stories rule society.'*
Plato

# 4

# Uses of YouTube
## Digital Literacy and the Growth of Knowledge

### YIRNing for YouTube

I invented YouTube. Well, not YouTube exactly, but something close - something called YIRN; and not by myself
exactly, but with a team. In 2003-2005 I led a research project
designed to link geographically dispersed young people, to
allow them to post their own photos, videos and music, and
to comment on the same from various points of view - peer to
peer, author to public, or impresario to audience. We wanted
to find a way to take the individual creative productivity that
is associated with the internet and combine it with the easy
accessibility and the openness to other people's imagination
that are associated with broadcasting, especially, in the context of young people, listening to the radio. So we called it
the Youth Internet Radio Network, or YIRN.[1]

As researchers, we wanted to understand how young people
interact as both consumers and producers of new media

content, especially of material made by their peers. We were also interested in the interface between non-market self-expression and commercial creative content (where music has always been exemplary). We wanted to trace the process by means of which individual creative talent may lead to economic enterprise and employment, and in general to understand how culture and creativity may be a seedbed for innovation and enterprise.

In order to find the answers to our research questions, we thought we would need to set up the appropriate website for young people to 'stick their stuff', which we would then observe by means of 'ethnographic action research' (Tacchi, Hearn & Ninan 2004), and if all went well we would make a contribution to rural and remote skills-development and regional sustainability. In the event, the workshops we held to train young people in techniques like digital storytelling did go well, but we spent two years failing to get the web interface right. Eventually we developed a site called *Sticky.net* ('a place to stick your stuff'), but by the time we'd fixed the functionality and solved the technical, design, security and IP issues the project was over, the kids had moved on and the site was barely populated. We had invented the idea of YouTube but failed to get it right in practice and in time, possibly because we were more interested in our research questions than in monetising consumer creativity. Well, that's what we told each other. Certainly it would have helped to be in the midst of mental California when the Zeitgeist, the kids and the technology happened to overlap. But we simply weren't.

YIRN was productive in the way that failure can be - it spawned quite a few bigger-and-better research projects in urban informatics, digital storytelling, youth creative enterprise and development communication, even if it didn't succeed in establishing a robust network for Queensland's creative youth. Later, as bandwidth finally expanded sufficiently to allow the internet to shift from text and music to video, YouTube 'proper' came along, with its simple slogan 'Broadcast Yourself', its easy usability (Flash), and its willingness to scale straight up, in no time flat, from 'me' (the first video being 'Me at the Zoo' by co-founder Jawed Karim) to 'global'. It was clear that neither Queensland youth nor anyone else needed their own special playground; much better to be part of a global commons where you might meet anyone. This is what YouTube quickly provided, and it taught me some lessons straightaway: that the open network is more important than anything else; that success comes from being in the right place at the right time; and that simplicity, ease of use and accessibility are more important than functionality, control or purposive direction.

Just as our funding ran out, YouTube was launched. Unlike us, it took off without displaying much interest in what the broadcast-yourself generation might want to use this newfound capability *for;* how it might be shaped towards imaginative, instrumental or intellectual ends. It simply . . . evolved (see Burgess & Green 2008).

But however successful YouTube has become, its evolution has left some questions unanswered. What do people need (to have, to know, to do) in order to participate in YouTube? Also, what results from just leaving it alone and letting learning happen by evolutionary random copying or contagion, rather than by 'disciplined' teaching? And what might be expected if 'we' - the users - decided to make a platform like YouTube useful not just for self-expression and communication but for description and argumentation too - for 'objective' as well as 'subjective' knowledge, in Karl Popper's terms (Popper 1972: chapter 3)?

When we set up YIRN we assumed that we needed to be active in the field of 'digital literacy'. We thought that you had to start by teaching users to make and upload content, and that you couldn't just leave them to their own devices as YouTube does. The downside of the YouTube model (of learning by doing and random copying) is that people don't necessarily learn what they need to express what they want. The upside is that very often they learn from each other, in the process of expanding the archive, and their efforts in turn teach others - just like YouTube celebrities 'Geriatric 1927' (Peter Oakley) or 'Tasha & Dishka' (Lital Mizel and Adi Frimmerman) of 'Hey Clip' fame. From this, more questions arise, about different models of education:

- Do new media of communication like YouTube and other internet affordances (open source programming, wikis, blogging, social networks, social bookmark folksonomies and the rest) require investment (public or private) in teaching whole populations how to use them? Or do they do better by blind experimentation and adaptation?
- Does the investment in the existing infrastructure of formal education have anything to offer? But if schools, colleges and universities are not the right vehicle, why not, and what is?
- Can we imagine a hybrid formal/informal (expert/ amateur; public/private) mode of propagation for learning 'digital literacy', and if so how might YouTube play a part?

- How might YouTube be exploited for scientific, journalistic and imaginative purposes as well as for self-expression, communication and file-sharing?

## Print to Digital Literacy

One way to address such questions is to compare digital literacy with its predecessor - print literacy. The nineteenth and twentieth centuries were notable for massive and sustained public investment in schools and (later on) universities - the infrastructure needed to deliver near-universal print literacy at low cost to the user. Right around the world the enormous cost was justified in order to produce modern citizens and a disciplined, skilled workforce for industrialisation. That effort has not been matched in the digital era. The physical ICT infrastructure that has developed since the 1990s for organisational, residential and lately mobile connectivity has not been matched by a concomitant investment in education - public or private - to promote its creative uptake and use by entire populations. Usage across different demographics is patchy to say the least, continuing to reproduce the class and demographic divides inherited from the industrial era. The scaling-up of digital literacy is left largely to entertainment providers seeking eyeballs for advertisers and to those who want consumers for their proprietary software applications; in other words, to the market.

If we are to believe what we read about Generation Y and 'digital natives', they are already in evolutionary mid-step. Today's high-school entrants - those who will be retiring from work around the year 2060 - seem almost a different species from modernists reared in the image of industry. Teens evidently don't see computers as technology. It's as if they have developed an innate ability for text-messaging, iPodding, gaming, and multitasking on multiple platforms. They can share their life story on Facebook, entertain each other on YouTube, muse philosophically in the blogosphere, contribute to knowledge on Wikipedia, create cutting-edge art on Flickr, and compile archives on Del.icio.us. Some can do most of these things at once, and then submit their efforts to an online ethic of collective intelligence and iterative improvability that is surely scientific in mode.

But they learn very little of this in school. For the most part the education system has responded to the digital era by prohibiting school-based access to digital environments including YouTube, apart from 'walled gardens' under strict teacher control.[2] From this, kids also learn that formal education's top priority is not to make them digitally literate but to 'protect' them from 'inappropriate' content and online predators. So a good many of them switch off and devote their energies to time-wasting, daydreaming and making mischief. However, as we saw in Chapter 1, daydreaming is just another word for identity-formation using individual imagination, and mischief is no more than experimental engagement with peer groups and places. Time-wasting (self-expression and social networking) has been the wellspring of the entertainment industry from time immemorial, supplying the characters, actions, plots and lyrics of fantasy fiction from *A Midsummer Night's Dream* to *I Know What You Did Last Summer.* Popular culture has prospered by capturing the attention, mood, time, activities and culture of young people (and others) in their leisure moments, when they're just beyond the institutional grasp of family, school or work. So while schools and universities keep their distance, *purposeless entertainment* has nurtured demand for creative self-expression and communication among the young.

Until recently, creative self-expression has been *provided* rather than *produced;* offered for a price on a take-it-or-leave-it basis by experts and corporations with little input by the consumers themselves. But now, with digital online media, there is almost infinite scope for DIY (do-it-yourself) and DIWO (do-it-with-others) creative content produced by and for consumers and users, without the need for institutional filtering or control bureaucracies. The so-called 'long tail' of self-made content is accessible to anyone near a computer terminal. Everyone is a potential publisher. Instead of needing to rely on the expertise of others, young people navigate themselves through this universe of information. Although schools and universities certainly teach 'ICT skills' and even 'creative practice', so far they have not proven to be adept at enabling demand-driven and distributed learning networks for imaginative rather than instrumental purposes.

Despite the democratising energies of advocates for literacy, and despite universal schooling, print-literate culture has resulted in a de facto division of labour between those who use print as an autonomous means of communication and those who use it - if at all - for private consumption. While most people can read, in print very few *publish*. Hence, active contribution to science, journalism and even fictional story-telling tends to be restricted to expert elites, while most of the population makes do with limited and commercialised 'uses of literacy', as Richard Hoggart pointed out half a century ago.

But the internet does not distinguish between literacy and publication. So now it is possible to imagine population-wide literacy in which everyone has the ability to contribute as well as consume. They can certainly use the internet for daydreaming and mischief - self-expression and communication - but it is quite possible to move on to other levels of functionality, and other purposes, including science, journalism and works of the imagination like the novel, those great inventions of print literacy, which must be transformed in the process. Despite misgivings among those with something to lose, these great realist textual systems do not have to be confined to authorised elites any more.

## Updating TV's 'Bardic Function'

Recently both business strategies and public-service thinking have stressed the need for organisations, governments and communities to evolve models of innovation that go beyond the closed expert process of the literate-industrial era. In a knowledge society, what is needed instead is an open innovation network. At the same time, the intuitive and imaginative skills of entrepreneurs in pursuit of 'creative destruction' and renewal can be compared with those of artists. The need for creativity in all aspects of economic and political life has been recognised. Creative talent commands economic as well as symbolic value. But an open innovation network benefits from harnessing the creative energies of the whole population, not just the inputs of isolated expert elites. With technologically enabled social networks using digital media, productivity can now be expected from consumers as well as producers, as users extend the growth of knowledge far beyond what can be achieved by professionals publishing in print. Hence, YouTube (among other online social networking sites), with all its unsystematic exuberance and unambitious content, devoted to no more than mucking around or, as the classic Hey Clip puts it, 'heya all! dancing stupid is fun',[3] is *simultaneously* the complex system in which digital literacy can find new purposes, new publishers and new knowledge. And anyone can join in, which ups the productivity of the whole system.

Thus far the commercial media and entertainment industries have pursued an industrial or expert-system model of production, where professionals manufacture stories, experiences and identities for the rest of us to consume. This system is 'representative', both in the sense that 'we' are represented onscreen and in the sense that a tiny band of professionals 'represents' us all. The productivity of this system is measured not by the number of ideas propagated or stories told but by the number of dollars earned per story. Thus, over the past century, cinema, radio and television have all organised and scaled human storytelling into an industrial system, where millions watch but mere hundreds do the writing. Broadcast media speak to and on behalf of us all in mass anonymous cultures.

This is the bardic function (Fiske & Hartley 2003; and see Chapter 3). Now that we can 'do it ourselves' - and 'do it with others' too - what might become of television's 'bardic function'? YouTube is the first large-scale answer to that question. Its slogan 'Broadcast yourself neatly captures the difference between old-style TV and new. YouTube massively scales up both the number of people *publishing* TV 'content' and the number of videos available to be watched. However, few of the videos are 'stories' as traditionally understood, not least because of radically reduced timeframes: ninety minutes for cinema; thirty to fifty minutes for TV, and one to two minutes for most YouTube. The best stories, for instance *lonely-girl15,* pretend to be something else in order to conform to the conventions of dialogic social networks.[4]

YouTube allows everyone to perform their own 'bardic function'. Just grab a harp (even an 'air harp')[5] and sing! With other social network enterprises, both commercial and community-based, it is a practical experiment in what a 'bottom-up' (all-singing, all-dancing) model of a 'bardic' system might look like in a technologically enabled culture. Instead of looking for a *social institution* or an *economic sector* like the original Celtic bardic order or the television industry, both characterised by expertise, restricted access, control, regulation and one-way communication, it is now possible to look for an *enabling social technology,* with near-ubiquitous and near-universal access, where individual agents can navigate large-scale networks for their own purposes, while simultaneously contributing to the growth of knowledge and the archive of the possible. The internet has rapidly evolved into a new 'enabling social technology' *for knowledge.* And just as 'new' media typically supplement rather than supplant their predecessors, it relies on both experts and everyone. It is the means by which 'bottom-up' (DIY consumer-based) and 'top-down' (industrial expert-based) knowledge-generation connects and interacts (Potts et al. 2008).

## YouTube Is Semiospherical

Human language is the primary model for this dynamic process of individuated productivity and action within an open complex system. Language, in general and in each distinct language, is only ever produced by individuals, but it expresses and connects a community as large in principle as all those who speak it, including the ones not yet alive who can read it later on, at least until it changes beyond recognition. A language is a network, but one of a special kind: what Albert-László Barabási (2002) has identified as a 'scale-free network':

> The brain is a network of nerve cells connected by axons, and cells themselves are networks of molecules connected by bio-chemical reactions. Societies, too, are networks of people linked by friendships, familial relationships and professional ties. On a larger scale, food webs and ecosystems can be represented as networks of species. And networks pervade technology: the Internet, power grids and transportation systems are but a few examples. Even the language we are using to convey these thoughts to you is a network, made up of words connected by syntactic relationships (Barabási & Bonabeau 2003: 50).

Barabási and Bonabeau (2003: 50) explain that scale-free networks are characterised by many 'nodes' with a few links to others in the network and a few 'hubs' with many links to other nodes. Complex networks appear to be organised by 'fundamental laws' that apply across to the physical, social and communicative worlds. Such discoveries have dramatically changed what we thought we knew about the complex inter-connected world around us. Unexplained by previous network theories, hubs offer convincing proof that various complex systems have a strict architecture, ruled by fundamental laws that appear to apply equally to cells, computers, languages and society. Such insights can begin to explain how individual points of origin and action are nevertheless linked into a coherent system, in which order emerges spontaneously and without the need for overall centralised control (Shirky 2008). Like language, the human network is itself networked, branched and differentiated. It can be understood both (anthropologically, structurally) as whole and (romantically, culturally) in its particulars.

The characteristics of complex adaptive systems apply to markets as well as to languages. Scale-free networks are characterised by *growth* (addition of new nodes), *preferential attachment* (new nodes seek links with already-linked hubs), and *hierarchical clustering,* where 'small, tightly interlinked clusters of nodes are connected into larger, less cohesive groups' (Barabási & Bonabeau 2003: 58).[6] It took the emergence of computational power to be able to model this kind of system mathematically, but that is now under way, in the economic sphere as well as in the 'enabling' sciences - particularly in evolutionary and complexity economics (Beinhocker 2006). Here the concept of 'preferential attachment' explains the principle of social network markets, whose special characteristic is that agents' choices (agents being both consumers and producers, both individuals and enterprises) are *determined by the choices of others* in the network (Ormerod 2001; Potts et al. 2008). Being able to see systems as whole and in terms of individual agency also has the effect, by the way, of reuniting the long-divergent 'two paradigms' (Hall 1980) of structuralism (system; whole) and culturalism (agency; particular) that have riven cultural studies since Raymond Williams.

The models that the network and scientists are coming up with look like language-models: a system in which nodes (agents/speakers) and relationships (links/communication) interconnect in an open complex network, coordinated by relatively few major hubs or 'institutions of language' including media organisations. This is Yuri Lotman's (1990) 'universe of the mind' - the 'semiosphere' - another name for which is 'culture'. When modelled mathematically, culture emerges not in *structured opposition* to economics (as cultural critics hold) but as part of the same *coordinated network*. YouTube is one such network.

## A Message from the Ancients

Much of human storytelling is 'said and done'. It is over with as soon as uttered, because most stories - most utterances - are part of what the linguist Roman Jakobson (1958) called *phatic* communication, checking the connection between speakers, not creating new knowledge. So most stories are ephemera, not archive. This function may predominate, along with emotive (self-expression) and conative (imperative) language use, among small, tightly connected clusters such as families and friends, in which each agent or node has few links and the message is uttered to maintain those links (thus phatic communication is sometimes called 'grooming talk'). This is why the internet has a lot of small-talk and chit-chat, and much less Shakespeare and science.

But some stories are not mere phatic exchange. Their function is not to connect the speakers but to describe the world or creatively to expand the system's capabilities. In Jakobson's terms, their function is not phatic but *referential* (information about the context), *poetic* (self-referential) or *metalinguistic* (about the code or system) (Jakobson 1958; see also Fiske & Hartley 2003: 62-3). Such stories may cumulatively become 'hubbed', with multiple links radiating across the network, playing a coordinating role. They might be myths, urban and otherwise, folklore or 'tales of yore'; or they might be retold in highly elaborated form, as song, drama or narrative. The point is that they retain innumerable points of origin (being retold afresh by all and sundry) but also a recognisable shape and coherence.

Writing about modern art in the context of the 'theatricality of ordinary behaviour', Goran Sonesson (2002) argues that, with the abolition of the modernist distinction between fine and popular arts in postmodernity, it is possible to see that fine arts borrow something new from popular arts, which themselves borrow it from ordinary life, namely the *phatic* function *as art:*

> Contemporary arts . . . repeat everyday, trivial situations, which have become standardised and repeatable, not because of the presence of some popular memory, but because of being projected over and over again by television and other mass-media: they exist thanks to the *bardic* function of television, as Fiske & Hartley call it, that is, in Jakobson's terms, thanks to the phatic function (Sonesson 2002: 24).

The argument here is that all three spheres of ordinary life, popular media and fine art are fully interconnected in a larger cultural network, and that art itself has reached the stage of development where it can recognise and gain inspiration from the most basic or banal functions of language. Although there is a lot of negative evaluation in public commentary on these matters, with banality, media, art and postmodernism all coming in for a good tongue-lashing, some important insights have been 'discovered' in this process: namely, that the *performance of the self is* just as coded, 'theatrical' and 'artistic' in ordinary life as it is in fine art; that subjectivity links power and aesthetics in performance; and that there is an open channel of mutual influence among these different hierarchical levels of the overall cultural network (manifested for instance in 'gossip' media and celebrity culture, where the attention accorded to celebrities like Paris and Britney is focused on their personal lives, which for others constitute the condition of ordinariness) (Hilton 2004).

As a result, it is possible to re-evaluate phatic communication itself. This is necessary in the context of digital media like YouTube, since so much of what is published in social network sites is phatic. To the modernist eye, trained in literate expertise, which seeks to minimise phatic utterances, it looks a proper mess. However, the problem here may be in the eye of the critical-literate beholder, not in the uses of the internet, for a medium in which phatic communication can be restored to full performative theatricality may also be restoring an ancient, multi-voiced mode of narration to cultural visibility. For example, Anil Dash, of Six Apart Ltd and an early adopter of blogging, has written:

> TV and newspapers and radio and books, especially in the West in the last 100 years, have dwindled down from a stream of thousands of concurrent parallel conversations to the serial streaming of the Big Six or Seven media companies. The train-of-thought, rambling, narrative tradition of human interaction which dates back to the earliest storytelling traditions of our species has been abandoned for bullet points (Dash 1999).

The implication of Dash's argument is that the web opens up 'public discourse' in a way that enhances ancient competences, which are distributed across the species, not restricted to the 'Big Six or Seven'. He argues that asides, interjections by third parties, annotation, hyperlinks and so on, all of which characterise YouTube as well as the blogosphere, add to the credibility, richness and critical value of a web-published document, which emerges not as a linear performance of the authorial self but as a concurrent performance of connectedness, collective intelligence and oral modes of storytelling. If this is so, then it is important to understand better the 'train-of-thought, rambling, narrative tradition of human interaction', because instead of dismissing it as phatic inconsequentiality, bad art or non-science it may be time to reappraise it as an intellectual resource. If storytelling - not to mention rambling - is an ancient resource, it may be wise to abandon invidious distinctions between different media, and to see them as part of the growth of knowledge, going back to the 'earliest storytelling traditions of our species'.

The cultural ubiquity of a restricted number of story-types, coming down from time immemorial, has led some to conclude that there is very little variety among plots. Joseph Campbell was a proponent of this view, proposing that a 'monomyth' runs as follows:

> A hero ventures forth from the world of common day into a region of supernatural wonder: fabulous forces are there encountered and a decisive victory is won: the hero comes back from this mysterious adventure with the power to bestow boons on his fellow man (Campbell 1949: 30).

The 'structural' analysis of myth and folklore also preoccupied the structuralists and formalists - Propp, Griemas, Todorov, Lotman and Bettelheim (Hawkes 1977).

More recently, Christopher Booker (2004) has identified seven basic plots that are structural transformations
of ancient tales:

1. Overcoming the Monster
2. Rags to Riches
3. The Quest
4. Voyage and Return
5. Rebirth
6. Comedy
7. Tragedy.

The most basic plot, 'overcoming the monster', which
characterises the oldest surviving story in the world, the
*Epic of Gilgamesh,* is also present in the classical stories
of Perseus and Theseus, the Anglo-Saxon poem *Beowulf,*
Culhwch and Olwen from the *Mabinogion,* 'fairytales' like
'Little Red Riding Hood', *Dracula,* and in contemporary
times H.G. Wells' *War of the Worlds,* or movies like *Seven
Samurai, Dr No, Star Wars: A New Hope* and *Jaws,* and
the 2007 3D-movie/anime hybrid *Beowulf.*

This kind of story is used to structure truth as well as fiction, news and politics as well as movies, and in exactly the
same way. Such narratives are part of what Robin Andersen
(2006) has called 'militainment'. A good example would
be the news coverage of George W. Bush's 'Mission accomplished' speech on board the USS *Abraham Lincoln* (1
May 2003), declaring both decisive victory in Iraq over 'a
great evil' - an unseen monster worthy of *Beowulf*'s Grendel
- and spelling out the boons bestowed by the heroes. The
final paragraph of the President's speech explicitly ties the
events of the day to 'a message that is ancient':

All of you - all in this generation of our military - have taken up the highest calling of history. You are defending your country, and protecting the innocent from harm. And wherever you go, you carry a message of hope - a message that is ancient, and ever new. In the words of the prophet Isaiah: 'To the captives, "Come out!" and to those in darkness, "Be free!"'[7]

Of course this story came back to haunt the Bush administration, but not because of its status as myth; it rebounded only because the monster wasn't dead - it wasn't a *good* story. Naturally the event was thoroughly clipped, spoofed and re-versioned on YouTube.[8]

## 'Those Who Tell Stories Rule Society' - Narrative Science

Christopher Booker's own method for discerning pattern in repetition was to read a lot of stories, and to explain the patterns in terms of Jungian archetypes, which he used to link stories to the process of individual 'self-realisation'. He also suggested that the science he was trying to found was long overdue:

One day, I believe, it will eventually be seen that for a long time one of the most remarkable failures of our scientific approach to understanding the world was not to perceive that our urge to imagine stories is something just as much governed by laws which lay it open to scientific investigation as the structures of the atom or the genome (Booker 2004: 700).

Reviewers were impressed with the laws, but less so with the enabling theory. Denis Dutton (2005), for instance, wrote:[9]

The basic situations of fiction are a product of fundamental, hardwired interests human beings have in love, death, adventure, family, justice, and adversity. These values counted as much in the Pleistocene as today, which is why they are so intensively studied by evolutionary psychologists.

Both Booker and Dutton are looking for ways of describing the coordinating mechanisms that allow individual agents not only to join the web of sense-making and hook up with other agents but also to reduce the potential infinity of experience, semiosis and structures to order, and in the process to achieve 'self-actualisation' (Abraham Maslow) if not 'self-realisation' (Carl Jung).[10] In other words, stories themselves are *organising institutions* of language and of self, simultaneously. *They* 'speak' the bards, the media and individual storytellers, rather than the other way around.

A network characterised by growth and change is dynamic, a 'scale-free' network:

> As new nodes appear, they tend to connect to the more connected sites, and these popular locations thus acquire more links over time than their less connected neighbors. And this 'rich get richer' process will generally favor the early nodes, which are more likely to eventually become hubs (Barabási & Bonabeau 2003: 55).

In the web of storytelling, Booker's seven basic plots are *hubs,* to which new events (plots) and agents (heroes) alike are 'preferentially attracted'. Thus new stories tend to end up like all the others:

1. **Anticipation stage:** *The call* to adventure, and the promise of what is to come.

2. **Dream stage:** The heroine or hero experiences some *initial success.* Everything seems to be going well, sometimes with a dreamlike sense of invincibility (what we might call the 'mission accomplished' stage).
3. **Frustration stage:** First *confrontation* with the real enemy. Things begin to go wrong.
4. **Nightmare stage:** At the point of maximum dramatic tension, disaster has erupted and it seems all hope is lost *(final ordeal).*
5. **Resolution:** The hero or heroine is eventually *victorious,* and may also be united or reunited with their 'other half' (a romantic partner).[11]

What is the benefit of reducing experience to such patterns? It may be that stories themselves are 'hard wired' to *enact* the sequence required for a new node to find productive links in a scale-free network. Stories are a *social technology* for passing on a model for how to navigate complex adaptive networks to succeeding generations. Stories are *about* how it feels and what it takes for a new 'node' to connect to a network, to navigate its topography, and to develop sufficient links to become a hub. There's a name for failure to connect too. Booker calls it 'tragedy'. And the name for characters who value *self over system?* Booker calls them 'evil'. Everything else is a version of Romance; they're all family dramas.

### Narrative Reasoning

Here storytelling does what science cannot. Eric Beinhocker (2006) reckons that stories are an evolutionary mechanism for *inductive reasoning:*

> As Plato said, 'Those who tell stories rule society'. . . Stories are vital to us because the primary way we process information is through *induction.* Induction is essentially reasoning by pattern recognition . . . We like stories because they feed our induction thinking machine, they give us material to find patterns in - stories are a way in which we learn (126-7).

Bearing in mind that this insight is offered in a book about complexity economics, it is as well to note that *learning* in this context is part of the answer to the question of how wealth is created, both long-term (evolutionary) and short-term (business success). Beinhocker is not celebrating the romance of the hero but seeking a scientific explanation for economic growth and an exact model for entrepreneurial action. In this context, learning has wealth-creating potential:

> Humans particularly excel at two aspects of inductive pattern recognition. The first is relating new experiences to old patterns, through metaphor and analogy-making . . . Second, we are not just good pattern recognizers, but also very good pattern-completers. Our minds are experts at filling in the gaps of missing information (127).

If Eric Beinhocker is right, and his is a very different model of 'economic rationalism' from that of traditional economics, then the stakes could hardly be higher. YouTube is a means for propagating this vehicle of inductive reasoning and learning to the outermost limit of the social; looking for ways to connect marginal, isolated, excluded or just shy 'nodes' so that they may thrive. He emphasises that we need to understand the 'micro-behaviors of individuals' in order to understand how the system as a whole works:

This model portrays humans as inductively rational pattern-recognizers who are able to make decisions in ambiguous and fast-changing environments and to learn over time. Real people are also neither purely self-regarding, nor purely altruistic. Rather, their behavior is attuned to eliciting cooperation in social networks, rewarding cooperation and punishing free riders (138-9).

This is what YouTube teaches too. Beinhocker goes on to say that 'networks are an essential ingredient in any complex adaptive system. Without interactions between agents, there can be no complexity' (141). In short, without such individual interactions, the entire system fails. So it behoves any progressive theory of communication to find a way to put the power of inductive reasoning - storytelling - where it belongs, in the minds and mouths of all agents, so that they may interact on a competitive footing, finding ways to 'access, understand and create communications in a variety of contexts', as one national media regulator defines 'media literacy'.[12] Thence they may learn to navigate the 'hierarchies of networks within networks' (Beinhocker 2006: 141) that characterise both markets in the global economy and meanings in the global sense-making system, including language, the internet - and YouTube.

*'Gawd! It looks like it could talk to me!'*
Olive Riley

# 5

# Digital Storytelling
## Problems of Expertise and Scalability
## in Self-Made Media

## Digital Storytelling

The term 'digital storytelling'[1] can be used generically to describe any computer-based narrative expression, including 'hypertext fiction' and game narratives as well as YouTube and the like. These developments have attracted an extensive literature, especially in relation to games. Here, however, the term refers only to the practice whereby 'ordinary people' participate in hands-on workshops using computer software to create short personal films that privilege self-expression; typically narratives of realisation of identity, memory, place and aspiration.[2] Digital storytelling fills a gap between everyday cultural practice and professional media that was never adequately bridged during the broadcast era (Carpentier 2003). Digital stories are simple but disciplined, like a sonnet or haiku, and anyone can learn how to make them. They reconfigure the producer/consumer relationship and show

how creative work by non-professional users adds value to contemporary culture (Burgess & Hartley 2004). A genealogy for this mode of digital storytelling has become established; it is a 'Californian export',[3] with some Welsh re-engineering, as will become clear below (Hartley & McWilliam (eds) 2009). This chapter considers two particular problems that the career of digital storytelling as a practice has continuously thrown up. The first is scalability. How can individual creative expression be scaled? Scalability has two aspects: (1) the bundling of stories, and (2) the propagation of the method of making them. The second problem concerns the delivery of digital storytelling workshops, typically by a professional expert compared with those who gather to learn and use the technique. The question of expertise therefore also has two aspects: (3) the role of the expert facilitator, and (4) the expertise of the user. The argument of this chapter is that solving these problems would translate digital storytelling from a phenomenon locked into the 'closed expert paradigm' to one active in an 'open innovation network'.

## Scale: Little or Large?

How is it possible to bundle *myriad self-made stories* in such a way that they are accessible to and valued by some larger group, whether that is understood as a community, a public, a market or a network? This is by no means an easy question to answer. Broadcasting and cinema completely failed to manage it. For many decades they didn't try to scale up *stories* because they were too busy scaling up *audiences*. Scale and organisation were focused around *distribution* rather than *production* (unlike in manufacturing industries). Although the publishing industry had evolved a business model in which *repertoire* and *backlist* (a sort of analogue long tail) allowed for an almost infinite extension of individual titles, time-based media like cinema and television never did 'scale up' their content beyond a few hours of new material per month (cinema) or per day (television, on a good day).

Although they were 'popular' in the sense that their content was widely noticed, broadcasting had a very limited 'supply side' that was not popular at all. Consumers did not supply stories to networks; networks supplied stories to consumers. Networks relied on (but also controlled) a highly specialised array of satellite production houses and trusted individuals. The 'market' in stories did not include consumers; it was organised around trade fairs in Los Angeles, Cannes and so on. As a result, *storytelling* became competitive and professional, undertaken by highly trained (and very lucky) experts. They heeded Wilkie Collins' (or was it Charles Reade's?) famous formula for fiction: 'make 'em cry, make 'em laugh, make 'em wait' (in that order). They reassured each other that there were only seven basic plots.[4] They knew what audiences liked and wanted. Oddly enough, this resulted in a culture that saw itself through the eyes of celebrities running away from explosions,[5] and could recognise friend from foe by the quality of their orthodontics (cinema has evolved from 'white hat vs black hat' to 'perfect teeth vs hideous teeth' - so it's OK to kill 'those awful orcs'). In other words, expert competition in a vertically integrated industry, with monopolistic tendencies rather than an open market, produces semiotic poverty, not choice.

Enter the internet. The stream of content-supply began to expand, to resemble first a telecommunications network and then a language community. So the question became: Is there something between the 'closed expert system' of traditional showbiz and the hive-like buzz of the internet that might allow individual voices to be voiced, bundled and distributed in such a way that they attract the attention of a significant number of other such individuals? In economic terms, was it possible to evolve from an 'industry' model of monopolistic control to an 'open market' model of exchange?

Is digital storytelling such a means? Early Utopian hopes suggested that it might hold just such possibilities. Here's Daniel Meadows:

> The promise of these big ideas for those of us formerly-known-as-the-audience is that we will be recast as the viewer/producers of a new participatory culture. Well, what I say is: 'Bring it on' (Meadows 2006).

How does digital storytelling 'bring it on'? It universalises the individual voice. It employs an aesthetic that seeks to balance democratic access (to both production and viewing) with communicative impact. Stories are around two minutes long, using voice-over scripts of around 250 words and a dozen still images, sometimes with video inserts. The idea is that a restricted palette facilitates the production of 'elegant' stories (Meadows' word) by people with little or no technical or aesthetic experience. The storyteller's unique voice is central to the process and is given priority in the arrangement of symbolic elements. Narrative accessibility, personal warmth and metaphysical 'presence' (Derrida 1976) are prioritised over formal experimentation or innovative uses of technologies (Burgess & Hartley 2004). The idea is that personal authenticity can reach out without sentimentality to touch others.

The first *problem* of scalability then is this: can enough stories be made and enjoyed by enough people for the form to sustain the level of ambition imagined for it by the pioneers - to be as democratic as speech, as connected as the internet and as compelling as . . . (say) . . . *Pan's Labyrinth?*[6] Current developments suggest that early ambitions have not been realised; in fact they've been scaled back. Imagined as an alternative to broadcasting, digital storytelling has been hard put to achieve the status of community media. Perhaps it has failed to spread because the requisite investment - public, private, intellectual - has not been made.

## Propagation: A Welsh Export?

The second problem of scalability is the propagation of the method. At the centre of digital storytelling is the workshop. It is labour-intensive, time-consuming and intimate, working best with about eight participants and one or two facilitators. It requires a fair amount of kit: one computer per person, plus cameras, sound-recording and editing packages. But more than this, it requires a *dialogic* approach to production, relying on a tactfully handled exploitation of a highly asymmetric relationship: the formal, explicit, professional, expert knowledge of the facilitator and the informal, tacit, 'amateur' or 'common' knowledge of the participant. *Both* are crucial to the exercise. The pedagogy most suited to this set-up is a Socratic method rather than the 'knowledge transfer' model beloved of technological fixers, from whose perspective the digital storytelling workshop must look costly and inefficient. For participants to make a successful story, the formal workshop element must call out their implicit or tacit knowledge, a process of 'outing' that aligns digital storytelling directly with the field of democratised innovation imagined by Charles Leadbeater (1999: 28-36).

Hence, the most important element of the workshops is not the training in computer use or editing but the so-called 'story circle' (Hartley & McWilliam 2009), a series of dialogic games in which people draw on their own and each other's embedded knowledge of stories, narrative styles, jokes and references. Much of this tacit knowledge is cultural rather than individual, of course, as witness the difference between age-cohorts observed in our workshops: older participants tended to emphasise facts and detail, linear time, an almost entirely referential use of images, and a journalistic tone; whereas the younger participants 'instinctively' used images metaphorically, in ways that provided a harmonic counterpoint to the spoken narrative, tended towards colloquial, everyday speech styles, and were more comfortable with the use of personal and emotive themes (Burgess & Hartley 2004).

Is digital storytelling a 'Californian export'? The Californian model - as I understand the tradition of Dana Atchley and Joe Lambert - is based loosely on *independent film practice,* in a tradition going back to Lenny Lipton in the 1970s and to the film workshop movement in British independent cinema (Lipton 1974), where individuals produce work for distribution via festivals or cultural institutions. This is an *artist + festival* model, often with a radically democratised notion of 'artist'.

In contrast, the model of distribution pioneered by Daniel Meadows in Wales, and imported into Australia by the Australian Centre for the Moving Image (ACMI) and QUT alike, is based not on arts festivals but on *broadcasting.* From the start, even though he learnt his digital storytelling at the feet of Dana Atchley, Meadows sought to associate his version of digital storytelling not with the film-festival circuit but with a broadcaster.[7] In the UK context that meant his funding/distribution agency was not the British Film Institute but the BBC. He experimented with various ways of incorporating the stories into TV and radio schedules as well as on the BBC website, innovations that are a significant component of his method of propagation.

The difference between Wales and California (both isolated on the western margins of metropolitan cultures, one in the rain, the other in the sun) reflects the fact that, unlike the United States (but like Australia and Europe), Wales has strong traditions of public-service broadcasting (PSB) and subsidised arts. PSB is available in Europe and Australia as a widely assimilated and institutionalised model of cultural practice, whereas the Californian model of 'independence' seems more libertarian and individualistic, based on music and film festivals under the stars in the desert. That is harder to emulate in Wales. Even so, Meadows' team has turned to a festival version of digital storytelling at Aberystwyth Arts Centre: at time of writing two such festivals (DSI 2006 and DS2 2007) had occurred. The DS2 festival blurb promotes it thus: DS2 aims to inspire, encourage, and show the exciting possibilities of Digital Storytelling whether you work in *education, the community or as an artist![8]* Heroic though such a venture may be, it might also signal that the *broadcasting* ambitions of digital storytelling in Wales have diluted, perhaps because it never received more than marginal support from the BBC, despite winning awards for them.[9]

The broadcast or Welsh variant of digital storytelling has been 'recaptured' by an amalgam of education and community arts. It has developed as a *cultural practice* rather than as a *media format.* Digital storytelling (the form) shows no sign of developing in the open market. Unlike YouTube (the platform), it is not visible as part of the general entertainment diet. It has not been commercialised; it is not owned or branded. It is neither 'hot' nor 'cool' in the 'economy of attention' (Lanham 2006). It does not share the ethic of iterative and collaborative knowledge like the Wikipedia or Creative Commons. Nor - despite Meadows' best endeavours - has it been adopted as part of PSB provision in countries with public-service and cultural institutions.

Digital storytelling does have something in common with existing initiatives in 'media literacy'. But its pioneers tend to be libertarians (on the Californian model) with an allergic response to formal schooling, so even in the context of schooling it has been taken up by activist educators inside the education system, rather than being pushed by 'digital storytelling entrepreneurs' as part of a societal distribution strategy in a 'social network' market. Thus, wherever digital storytelling has taken root, a publicly assisted cultural or educational institution is usually involved.

Unresolved questions remain, therefore, as to whether the digital storytelling *form* is better suited to distribution via festival, broadcasting or network, and whether the *method* can succeed without relying on the resources of education or community arts/media organisations. At QUT those resources were crucial; without them the university could not have 'imported' Daniel Meadows himself. He came several times in 2003-2005 to offer masterclasses and to 'train the trainers'; the trainers were generally researchers who wanted to deploy the workshops in youth or community development R&D

initiatives, but there were also academics who introduced digital storytelling into degree-level teaching. Meadows trained two groups from QUT, who in turn went on to adapt the technique in projects supported by the Australian Research Council, QUT itself, and various state agencies.

How can digital storytelling - as a 'method' to 'bring it on' - be propagated throughout the community? Social networking sites like YouTube skip formal tuition and encourage users to go straight to online publishing (or archiving), which itself differs from publishing 'as such' by being much more in the here-and-now and part of a conversation, resulting in many more 'anthropological' postings ('raw' videos from everyday life, like Bus Uncle),[10] as well as rip-offs, mash-ups and tribute vids from other media. Digital storytelling, on the other hand, requires bandwidth and bundling, and it also needs to be taught. It requires a workshop, especially (but not only) for people who are currently inactive in relation to digital media. The finished product is generally a big file that is shared among people already formed into a community - but not a public - like family, friends or an interest group. It is propagated via local organisations, cultural institutions and activist agents (like education and art). Compared with other exports such as YouTube, My Space and Wikipedia, that doesn't seem very 'Californian'. However, YouTube is available (as it was not when digital storytelling was invented) as a platform for stories generated elsewhere, so there is no need to see them as opposed 'business models'.

Even so, digital storytelling is not 'native' to the internet, and it is yet to develop efficient means of distribution or self-sustaining growth (as against blogs, for example). Nor does it readily exploit some of the more innovative capabilities of the internet, for instance iterative content, open to reuse and re-appropriation by other users. Digital stories are relatively closed texts (that is, not hypertexts) (Burgess & Hartley 2004). They are bandwidth-intensive, so they are currently more easily propagated by DVD than by download: there's a 'handmade' or 'manuscript' feel to them even when they appear on websites (e.g. Capture Wales).[11] If digital storytelling is to gather its own momentum and to play a significant role in public culture, the next step is to move beyond the focus on production at the local level, however much the participants benefit from being part of the workshops, and however much the cultural institutions benefit from engaging members of the community as co-creators. Digital storytelling needs to address the question of how to scale up content for audiences, and how to propagate the method as part of universal education (though not as *schooling!*). This step leads to the problems of expertise.

## The Expert: Bully or Pulley?

Turning to expertise, the first problem here is the role of the facilitator in the production of self-made media. Often motivated by both artistic and political considerations, the facilitator is in a position analogous to that of the documentarist, with a community-arts educator (or *animateur*) thrown in. Why is that a problem? It's a problem because *self-made* media ought not to need input from the expertise of someone external to the self whose story is being narrated. And we have the example of YouTube to show that hundreds of millions of users (and climbing) don't need it. Can 'ordinary people' successfully get on with what they want to do when their hand is being held, however 'helpfully', by a well-meaning facilitator?

In documentary this is a problem that goes back many decades to Flaherty,[12] Grierson[13] and *cinema verité*[14] in cinema, and the same applies to still photography too, where the rights and role of the 'subject' have long been in dispute. So that is the most obvious problem: you think you're going out there to empower Florrie and Nora; but you come back with *Night Mail.* Indeed, such 'documentary' endeavours often look highly authored, no matter how strong the voice of the subject. For instance, the entirely authentic stories catalogued on the *Capture Wales* site nevertheless 'speak' of Daniel Meadows (himself a noted documentary photographer since the 1970s). How can untutored populations 'speak for themselves'?

This is part of a larger problem. In general, across industrial cultures the 'expert paradigm' has been an impediment to the development of self-made meaning and self-representation by lay populations. Any *representative* system (including both politics and cinema) tends to discourage direct participation, even while it piles up honour and reward for the representatives and experts. Whether it is in the mode of production (e.g. the making of TV/film and entertainment) or in political participation (journalism, politics), the *closed expert system* has produced a serious gulf between the high level of talent among the best *'practitioners'* and the impoverished 'media literacy' of the *punters.*

And there's the rub. Work produced by the imaginative elite is excellent by any standard; it is granted that status not least by the approval and enthusiasm of the punters themselves. So when experts do seek to facilitate the 'universal' voice of individual humans, the result can be brilliant. Such experts include Dana Atchley and his Californian compadres, Daniel Meadows and his Welsh wizards, not to mention the film documentarists, among whom I personally place Humphrey Jennings at the top. Jennings used ordinary people to illustrate larger themes. His 1943 propaganda film *The Silent Village*[15] is an early example of 'pro-am' or interactive production in the making of movies; what might now be called 'consumer co-creation'. His own skills and passions were vital to the enterprise, but they were successfully subsumed into the service of a greater work, one which cast the ordinary citizen as actor - an actor in history as well as in the film. He turned the major mass medium of his day into a means of communication for its own consumers to send a message of hope across the world. The result is great *collaborative art* imagining genuinely *popular culture* (see Hartley 2006 for a full account of this earlier Welsh export).[16]

So the *problem* of the expertise of the facilitator - turning the 'authenticity' of others into the 'authorship' of the expert - would not be solved by simply firing all the filmmakers and letting consumers get by on their own. It is important not to fall for an 'either/or' model of digital storytelling: either *expert* or *everyone*. Instead of choosing between the expert paradigm and self-expression, objective and subjective knowledge, it would be preferable to hold fast to both. To do that, it is necessary to abandon the linear model of communication and to replace it with one founded in dialogue:

> Human intelligence . . . cannot switch itself on by itself. For an intelligence to function there must be another intelligence. Vygotsky was the first to stress: 'Every higher function is divided between two people, is a mutual psychological process'. Intelligence is always an interlocutor (Lotman 1990: 2).

According to Yuri Lotman, the development of 'human intelligence' is necessarily dialogic; everyone is an 'interlocutor', even when expressing their 'inner self'. This applies to digital as well as to oral and print communication. It follows that there will be uneven competences, ambitions and levels of 'literacy' in play, but also that dialogue is still possible. Indeed, Lotman argues that what he calls 'bipolar asymmetry of semiotic systems' is the generative mechanism of meaning in any semiotic system, from single texts to languages and culture (that is, everything from mother/infant 'language of smiles' to the reception-transmission turn-taking between entire cultures, for instance Russian/French):

> It has been established that a minimally functioning semiotic structure consists not of one artificially isolated language or text in that language, but of a parallel pair of mutually untranslatable languages which are, however, connected by a 'pulley', which is translation. A dual structure like this is the minimal nucleus for generating new messages, and it is also the minimal unit of a semiotic object such as culture (Lotman 1990: 2).

Lotman's model is helpful for understanding the role of the expert as a 'translator', especially for those who are culturally 'monoglot' when it comes to literacy — that is, they have print literacy but not media or digital literacy (and vice versa). In digital storytelling there is a clear asymmetry between facilitator and participant, but it doesn't have to be construed in terms of differential *power* (Gibson 2007). Instead, it invokes that most important attribute of the literary translator, which is not only knowledge of the technical aspects of both the home 'language' and the target 'language' but also (ideally) a wide knowledge of their literary, journalistic, scientific and popular-cultural elaborations, and a facility for translating the strengths of one into the strengths of the other, even where there is 'mutually untranslatable' asymmetry. In short, the expertise of the filmmaker or documentarist when coupled with a 'parallel' intelligence from the lay population can result in new and compelling stories that do credit to both parties.

**Expertise: 'Gawd! It Looks Like It Could Talk to Me!'**

Among the successors of Humphrey Jennings is Australian filmmaker Mike Rubbo. Rubbo came to international prominence with *Waiting for Fidel* (1974),[17] which is said to have inspired Michael Moore's style. He has released films in every decade since the 1960s, recently winning an AFI Award for *Much Ado About Something* (2001).[18] But it was as 'Mike the helper' that he figures in this story. In 2006 Rubbo made a documentary called *All About Olive* for ABC-TV, featuring Olive Riley, who was 107 years old. Later he assisted Olive to produce her own blog - *The Life of Riley*[19] - in which she claimed to be the world's oldest blogger. A typical entry was 'It's a Likeness', the story of Olive going to have her portrait painted, an adventure that included the trip to the studio, a parking ticket and a pie, recorded in transcribed dialogue and still photos by Rubbo. When Olive saw the finished portrait she exclaimed: 'Gawd, it looks like it could talk to me!',[20] which was a good epithet for her blog. The site attracted worldwide attention and high levels of visits (192,000 in the first month), along with many comments (nearly 500 on the first three entries in February 2007). The format was that Rubbo recorded dialogue with Olive and typed it up, interspersed with photos old and new, and with occasional commentary in italics from 'Mike the helper'. The result was a new hybrid form - part blog (since it used the first person although it is written by someone else), part digital storytelling transcript, part multiplatform publishing. Rubbo replied to almost every comment posted on the site, maintaining a conversation that extended the themes of Olive's current adventure and producing new information or photographs to share with the community of interest that gathered around Olive. Presumably because of Rubbo's own media savvy, the 'oxygen of publicity' included both press and broadcast coverage. Some of this was also used to solicit participation by others (e.g. appealing for photos of places in Olive's life), which in turn attracted visitors to the site, including those who had seen press coverage in Poland, the United States, the United Kingdom, Germany and so on.

A notable feature was that Rubbo - who was himself nearing seventy years old at this time - was no more a 'digital native' than Olive. He was an expert filmmaker with a fine documentary sensibility, but computers were another matter. He shared his learning curve with visitors, explaining to one why he did not podcast his conversations with Olive: 'Just getting this far, pictures and words, has been an effort. I'm going to need help with podcasts. I'm a senior too and way out of my previous comfort zone already. Mike the helper.'[21]

Rubbo's position as a 'helper' showed how professional expertise could be deployed in a convivial way. It demonstrated how the asymmetrical relationship between expert (Rubbo) and first-person storyteller (Olive) can produce something new that stretches both of them. Meanwhile, the blog and its associated media coverage called a sizable 'conversational public' into being, for whom the personal contact with Olive and side-bar chats with Rubbo were both of value. It was a multiplatform 'open innovation network' in miniature.

The Riley-Rubbo mode of digital storytelling developed by happenstance, not by workshop, and its one-to-one relationship between facilitator and user would be hard to replicate, let alone scale up. But it does point the way towards a 'dialogic' development of expertise among users, based on a conversational ethic and 'parallel intelligence' applied to concrete but nevertheless objective issues. Olive's blog actively produced and shared new expertise among all parties. It helps us to visualise a digital storytelling 'system' in which producer-citizens who are doing it for themselves can build their own expertise, call in that of others, and use their new-found 'digital literacy' to do previously unimagined things (unimagined by the expert providers of mainstream media and by consumer-users themselves, especially as individuals).

This means that digital storytelling is not an end in itself but part of a larger cultural process, which may be 'natural' but also needs effort, both to *extend the users* of digital literacy across whole populations, and to *elaborate the uses,* so as to democratise public engagement with digital media, and to contribute generally to the growth of knowledge, especially of the kinds most suited to digital media. It is only one step along the way, because to date it has been concerned almost exclusively with 'first-person' narratives; stories of identity, emotion and self-realisation. Fair enough, but there's more to language than self-expression and communication: there is also knowledge. In fact, the philosopher Karl Popper (1972) has produced a typology of the 'levels' of language:

1. Self-expression
2. Communication

3. Description
4. Argumentation (chapter 3).

For Popper, the first two levels produce subjective knowledge; the second two can lead to objective knowledge. For us, it is noteworthy that digital storytelling, in common with the media-entertainment complex in general, is obsessively focused on the first level. To take a further step towards the two 'higher' levels of language, the question of expertise needs to be pressed: how can everyone in a given community be in a position to contribute to the growth of objective knowledge? Here print literacy is an instructive antecedent. Over a long timeframe (the seventeenth century to the nineteenth century in Europe), print literacy escaped from instrumental purposes like religion, business and government, to become a culture-wide capability. It is worth noting that this was possible only because of massive *public* investment in schooling, whose aim was universal print literacy. But what it could be used *for* also escaped the institutional and individual purposes of the early proselytisers. As a social resource - a form of embedded human capital - print literacy enabled science, literature, journalism and entertainment. The Enlightenment, modernity, industrialisation and mass media were all founded on it. What will be the forms of expertise that grow up among those who take for themselves the power of self-expression in digital media? That's the second problem of expertise.

**Digital Storytelling for Science, Journalism, Imagination?**

Karl Popper has linked the evolution of objective knowledge, and thence science, modernity and the open society, to the invention of printing. This is one reason why universal education was thought wise. It is worth asking whether the invention of digital media may be enabling a further evolutionary step in the growth of knowledge. If so, two things need to happen.

First, the 'ordinary people' - the punters, the participants, the inexpert consumers - need to be able to develop and share expertise of their own (and their own expertise), such that they too can contribute to the life of science, imagination and journalism, as well as that of self-expression and communication. In other words, Olive's experiential and tacit knowledge of places and themes are interesting in themselves, but, especially when taken up by her interlocutors, they are also capable of producing new 'objective' knowledge, for instance about places where she has lived, filling in the historical and archival record in ways that local galleries and libraries value. This is Lotman's 'parallel intelligence' in the realm of knowledge: uniting subjective and objective, experience and expertise, in dialogic asymmetry.

The second thing is that digital storytelling needs to be used for more than self-expression and communication. Digital media need to be exploited to generate new 'objective' description, new argumentation (Popper's negative or falsifiable method of scientific enquiry); and while we're at it, new forms of journalism and new works of the imagination too. Of course, all of this is already happening; choose your own favourite examples. The general point is that such initiatives need to be understood coherently as an *extension* of the possibilities of knowledge, even while their experiential self-expression is an assault on the closed expert system as such. The emancipation of large numbers of otherwise excluded (or neglected) people into the 'freedom of the internet' will, if successful and if pushed beyond a 'look at me' stage, assist not only in self-expression and communication but also in the development of knowledge in an open innovation network. Digital storytelling is an excellent initiative for recruiting new participants into that open network, and for lifting levels of digital literacy and popular expertise. It may be modelling for the coming century the role - if not the methods - of public schooling in the early period of print literacy.

But it shouldn't be seen as an end in itself, as if knowledge of the personal is all that is necessary for people outside of the existing professional elites. It is no advance to reinforce the barriers between popular culture and expert culture; to *substitute* 'self' for 'science'. The consequences of doing that are already part of the crisis confronting contemporary societies. The cultivation of the personal as a sufficient ambition for the majority (while those 'in the know' disappear behind closed institutional doors) can lead to the very evils of relativism that experts rail against, encouraging the general public to believe that anything goes, that knowledge is only a matter of opinion, or that self-expression is the highest form of communication. Cutting people off from it means that despite the wonders of science the punters are more sceptical about it than ever. As the late Kurt Vonnegut once put it, 'I began to have my doubts about truth after it was dropped on Hiroshima' (Vonnegut 1981: 223). Not only are the fruits of scientific research often rejected or delayed in the court of public opinion - GM foods, nuclear energy, global warming - but even the underpinning commitment to rationality and the open society are being 'white-anted' from within by resurgent religiosity, a 'me' culture and a politics of fear.

The need is not to separate 'science' (description and argumentation) and 'popular culture' (self-expression and communication) further from one another but to find ways of holding them together. At the moment the way that professional scientists tend to do this is by speaking very slowly and clearly (public understanding of science) or ventriloquising through celebrities and pop-stars (Bono). The expert paradigm is still in place; maybe more so as more expert intermediaries are hired to 'manage' public knowledge.

Meanwhile, over in popular culture, knowledge has been growing all by itself. The shift from broadcast to interactive media in particular has democratised self-expression and complicated the entire edifice of 'representation' in both symbolic and political communication. We are no longer satisfied with deferring to representatives; we want direct voice, action, creative expression - and, increasingly, knowledge. If the problems of scalability and expertise are well-handled, digital storytelling can play a progressive role in this endeavour, not by pandering to the metaphysics of individual presence or by convincing the public of the expertise of others but by democratising both self-expression and expertise, such that presently unthought-of innovations can occur in the growth of knowledge, and the general public can join the life of science, imagination and journalism, as well as that of self-expression and communication.

# 6

# A Writing Public
## Journalism as a Human Right

### Cultural Studies and Journalism

Cultural studies and journalism overlap in important respects. They are both interested in the mediation of meanings through technology in complex societies. Both investigate ordinary everyday life: journalism from the point of view of reportable events, cultural studies from that of ordinary lived experience. They both display eman-cipationist tendencies: journalism as part of the modern tradition of liberal freedoms, cultural studies as part of a critical discourse developed around struggles over identity, power and representation. But the tradition of journalism *research* that has grown up within university programs has tended to focus less on the overall purpose of journalism in modern societies and more on its purpose as a profes-sional occupation in an industrialised and corporate mode of production (Gans 2004). Cultural approaches have played only a minor role in this tradition. Indeed there is a tendency for cultural and journalistic approaches to be seen as either adversarial or mutually exclusive, despite (or because of) the fact that they share a common interest in the communication of meaning within societies characterised by conflict (Green & Sykes 2004).

This chapter seeks to perform as well as to describe a cultural approach to journalism. It opens with an account of how 'cultural studies' has approached journalism as an object of study. It is the overall approach - which is critical, not quantitative - that is important, rather than any specific set of research findings. The chapter goes on to perform a cultural approach by proposing that journalism should not be seen as a professional practice at all but as a human right.

## The Cultural Approach to Journalism

Cultural studies emerged in the 1960s as a critical, intellectual and educational enterprise. Its purpose was critical, not professional. It was founded on teaching, not research. As an oppositional discourse it was not devoted to improving the expertise of practitioners; it sought to empower *readers and audiences,* not journalists. Therefore, journalism research performed on behalf of the profession, or for news organisations or as part of the PR industry was not its main priority.

British cultural studies (Turner 2002; Lee 2003) grew directly out of a perceived inadequacy of modern frameworks of knowledge, whether disciplinary (e.g. political science, economics, sociology and literary studies) or activist (e.g. Marxism), to explain how social change occurred or how it could be encouraged, and for whose benefit. Existing frameworks were based on *economics* and *politics,* characterising the human 'subject' of modernity as the *worker* and the *voter,* and focusing emancipationist struggles on the workplace via the labour movement and trade unionism (economics) and the ballot box via Labour parties in parliaments (politics). But by the mid-twentieth century neither of these struggles had precipitated the predicted social transformation and popular emancipation.

Meanwhile, established explanations of the role of culture in society (e.g. literary studies) seemed to ignore culture's impact on both economic and political developments, focusing instead on aesthetic matters. Culture was seen by modernist political and economic analysts as an epiphenomenon, an effect rather than a cause of change, and by modernist cultural theorists as an antidote to the political and economic direction of the day rather than an engine of it. For literary-based approaches, the 'subject' of modernity was not the worker or the voter but the *reader.*

There was a split between politico-economic and literary-aesthetic approaches to culture, which found institutional form in the division between the social sciences and the humanities. It is noteworthy that journalism programs in higher education are to be found on both sides of that divide. Early college-based journalism training schemes were largely literary (Hartley 1996: 247-8), their purpose being to turn out professional writers. But journalism programs are now likely to be located in social science faculties (somewhere between communications and business) or in departments of politics and government. Journalism research is the progeny of these disciplines.

The project of cultural studies too was to integrate the economic (worker), political (voter) and cultural (reader) spheres as a coherent object of study, and to investigate why and how culture may affect the apparently determinant spheres of economics and politics. If working-class people didn't behave as their economic and political class interests dictated they should, was there something about their culture that promoted conformism or could promote change? Was culture - after all - *causal* (Williams 1961)?

It was at this point that cultural analysts interested in social change started to look in detail at the concept of subjectivity, shifting attention from *the worker* and *the voter* (or masses) to *the consumer* in the communicative form of *audiences.* In order to understand why social change did not follow from activism at the factory gate or via the ballot box, the impact of industrialised forms of communication (popular publishing, newspapers, cinema and broadcasting) on the subjectivity and consciousness of popular readers and audiences was quickly identified as a potential stumbling block. Was journalism, which from its own perspective was a beacon of liberal-democratic freedom, in fact an impediment to the emancipation of classed, raced, gendered and otherwise 'othered' subjects? Was the nightly news part of an apparatus of power and control (Hall et al. 1978; Ericson, Baranek & Chan 1987)?

The cultural approach to journalism was interested in the subjectivity of readers and audiences of popular media in order to assess the ideological, political and economic impact of news media, as part of the apparatus of global corporate communications. However the social-science/humanities disciplinary divide kicked in again here. The structural and institutional aspects of that apparatus - the operations of the state, corporations and power-elites - were taken up in studies of the political economy of the culture industries, news media among them. Some critics have regarded political economy as part of the project of cultural studies, while others have seen it as a distinct tendency (Miller (ed.) 2001). Meanwhile, cultural analysts have drawn on literary, linguistic and semiotic traditions to investigate how subjectivity is fixed in language, and how unequal power relations in modern societies are conducted on a day-to-day basis, both in everyday life and via the mass media. They were interested in the production and circulation of meaning in society, in order to answer this question: if power operates to 'subject' people in various ways, how is it done communicatively? How is power transmitted through texts like newspapers and television broadcasts? This led to the practice of 'critical readings' or 'demystification' of media texts including journalism (Hartley 1982). The cultural approach to journalism has therefore been interested from the start in the *textual* relations between a powerful 'addresser' (media corporations, government agencies) and emancipation-seeking 'addressees' (audiences, readers). Such textual relations of 'encoding' and 'decoding' (Hall 1973; Hall, Connell & Curti 1977) were investigated in detail to try to understand how meaning was conveyed or constructed in large-scale media, what some of the dominant meanings were, and what needed to be done to emancipate subordinate groups from being 'subject' to them.

Cultural studies' founding interest in economic and political determinants of change entailed a focus on social class, especially the working class, but over time this extended to gender, ethnicity, race, first peoples, sexual orientation, nation, age-group, and to identities formed around taste-cultures like music (mods, punk) or fanship (Trekkies). This attention to identity among consumers and audiences in popular culture has produced much of what is recognised as cultural studies.

Journalism *as such* was not its object of study. However, it was in the context of identity politics that user-led and consumer-created journalism first became a significant topic, via the zines of subcultures and countercultures, and the counterpublic spheres proclaimed in the feminist, anti-war and environmental movements (Felski 1989).

Journalism was incorporated into cultural studies not as a *professional* practice but as an *ideological* practice. News texts (including photos and audiovisual forms of reporting) were analysed for their semiotic, narrative and other communicational properties, in order to identify what causes the political or social impact that critics believe they have observed, and what resources ordinary people may have or build to resist the same, or to pose and create alternatives. The context of reception is as important in this assessment of journalism as is the context of production. That context is seen as a community (culture), not a market (economics) or a constituency (politics).

The cultural approach to journalism is not a disciplinary project and is not associated with an agreed methodology. Because of its heterogeneous and interdisciplinary nature, one of its distinctive features over the years has been 'reflexivity', which in brief means recognising the position of the investigator both politically and as a knowing-subject. Indeed, it is an interventionist form of analysis; its proponents want to change the world, not merely to understand it; many of its writers seek to produce activists.

## The Challenge of 'Everyone'

In order to perform - reflexively - the cultural approach, and to show that the universalist ambitions of liberal journalism can be integrated with the emancipationist claims of cultural studies, the rest of this chapter takes up the challenge of the bold hypothesis advanced in Article 19 of the UN Universal Declaration of Human Rights (UDHR), especially that of the radically Utopian-liberal idea that 'everyone' - no exceptions! - has the right not only to seek and receive 'information and ideas' but to *'impart'* (communicate) them:

> *Article 19:* Everyone has the right to freedom of opinion and expression; this right includes freedom to hold opinions without interference and to seek, receive and impart information and ideas through any media and regardless of frontiers (UN 1948).

As the influential British journalist and editor Ian Hargreaves has also put it:

> In a democracy everyone is a journalist. This is because, in a democracy, everyone has the right to *communicate* a fact or a point of view, however trivial, however hideous (Hargreaves 1999: 4).

Hargreaves' real challenge, like that of the UDHR itself, is to society at large. But it is also a challenge to journalists and journalism educators, and therefore to journalism research. If *'everyone* is a journalist', how can journalism be *professed?* If its real extent is 'everyone in a democracy', then journalism research needs to extend its horizons beyond the occupation of journalist or the news industry as presently constituted.

If 'everyone is a journalist', there is a challenge to cultural studies here too. For the *consumer* (reading public) is transformed into the *producer* (journalist). What happens when the 'reading public' (audience or consumer) of modernity turns into the 'writing public' (user, 'prosumer' or ProAm') of global interactive media (Leadbeater & Miller 2004, Bruns 2005)?

## Journalism as an Ethnicity

Until recently, the means have not been available to turn the UDHR's universal human right into a right that can be exercised by humans in general. Instead, *journalism* has exercised that right on behalf of the public. In representative democracies we have grown used to 'representative journalism' - our freedom to impart is exercised by journalists on everyone's behalf (in the public interest). Like representative politics, this has become an increasingly professionalised, corporatised and specialised occupation, and increasingly remote from the common life and lay population it represents.

Meanwhile, journalism has grown up throughout the modern period as an occupation with a strong culture of separation between insiders and outsiders. Indeed, what with their 'nose for news', their 'gut feeling' for a story, and the idea that good journalists are 'born not made' (Given 1907: 148), there is a sneaking suspicion that journalism may be experienced by insiders more as an *ethnicity* than as a human right. Indeed, journalists are beginning to conform to the definitional status used in Australia and elsewhere to identify Aboriginal people: to qualify as such, you need to (1) be descended from, (2) identify and live as, and (3) be accepted by a particular community which wants to recognise, preserve and transmit its unique cultural heritage (ADAA 1981: 8). In their own eyes, journalists are literally a tribe.

A corollary of this distinction between journalism's 'we' community and its outside is that journalism research is routinely confined to the study of the insider perspective. Journalism education, likewise, means training for jobs in existing newsroom organisations. Few if any journalism schools educate for journalism as a human right; but many assume that anyone who hasn't practised journalism as a newsroom employee is not competent to profess journalism, nor should they be allowed to educate those for whom it will become a primary occupation. The result of this is that journalism research and education have become part of a *restrictive practice.* They are designed to keep outsiders *out* of journalism.

It may be protested at this point that that is a highly desirable situation, because journalists ought to be trained to high standards, and entry into the profession ought to be restricted to those who can do a good job, as in other professions like medicine and the law. That is a persuasive argument, but unfortunately it conforms neither to the facts of journalism as practised in many countries (where the way someone looks can trump good training) nor to the interests of societies that espouse individual freedom and liberal democracy. The societal objection to professionalism is that restricting journalism to those who have qualified by whatever process is tantamount to licensing the expression of ideas, which is simply anti-democratic. In some countries, training itself is viewed with suspicion by editors, owners and even many senior journalists, for whom it is not a profession but a trade to be learnt on the job. As a result, it is still possible to work as a journalist without any professional training. At the same time, the majority of journalism graduates do not go on to work in newsrooms. The laudable desire to have competent practitioners and an explicit understanding of the practice is directly at odds with both industry and democratic imperatives.

Journalism schools' own consumers, meanwhile, suggest a very different possibility. Many undergraduates take journalism degrees as a new form of the general arts degree, one with practical skills and engagement with political and business applications. They may have no intention of gaining entry to the (increasingly bureaucratised and proletarianised) corporate newsroom. They are already acting as though everyone is a journalist, and honing some critical skills without wanting to 'be' journalists.

## Journalism as a Transitional Form

Scholarship about the production side of news has obscured the fact that, despite its longevity (about four hundred years), journalism 'as we know it' may be a *transitional form,* constructed on the technical impossibility of achieving its full democratic potential, namely that *everyone* has a right to *practise* it. During the mechanical and broadcast phases of modernity, journalism depended on the printing press or electronic media production techniques, where increasingly heavy capital investment was needed to achieve wide-scale reach and ratings. It developed a *one-to-many* model of *mass* communication, the antithesis of the right to individual freedom of expression which it purported to represent.

But now the interactive phase of modernity has begun to take technical shape and unsurprisingly journalism has become one of the first victims of post-broadcast interactive media, starting with the internet (Matt Drudge)[1] but quickly burgeoning to encompass various user-led forms regardless of the technological platform, including e-zines, blogging and what Axel Bruns (2005) calls 'collaborative' online journalism. Journalism has transferred from modern expert system to contemporary open innovation - from 'one to many' to 'many to many' communication.

So, out with journalism as an ethnicity, and in with journalism as a human right. If journalism is a *human* right, then it is necessary not only to theorise it as a craft that everybody can practise but also to extend what counts as journalism beyond the democratic-process model to encompass much more of what it means to be human; especially the world of private life and experience, and the humanity of those lying outside the favoured gender, ethnic, national, age or economic profiles that are targeted by corporate news media. Such an eventuality has been thoroughly rehearsed, as it were, in the alternative and social-movements media, the underground or countercultural press, community broadcasting, fanzines, and also in cultural or entertainment forms of mainstream journalism, including fashion, lifestyle, consumer and leisure reporting (Lumby 1999). These forms employ many of the world's journalists, but they barely rate a mention *as journalism* in journalism schools, which remain wedded to watchdog, fourth estate or First-Amendment models of journalism as the representation - and representative - of the democratic process (Gans 2004), and are concomitantly dismissive of non-news or lifestyle journalism, which is equated with feminised consumption and for that reason despised.

## Journalism and Culture

Research into journalism as a human right, a *general capacity for communicative action,* has not yet been established. But it too has been rehearsed, in a branch of inquiry that focuses on the media consumer and the context within which the commodity form of news is taken up into people's everyday lives to become culture. This is, in fact, the very place where cultural studies first came in (Hoggart 1957; Hall et al. 1978). Cultural approaches to journalism start where the latter becomes *meaningful*. They are interested in the moment when political economy, textual system, cultural form and ideology converge on the point of consciousness, the point where cultural identities are forged in an alloy of symbolic and economic values. Cultural studies wants to know what journalism means in the context of its social and cultural uptake. But in contemporary society (mechanico-electronic modernity) journalism as a *practice* is separated from journalism as *meaning*. There has thus been a division of intellectual labour, where journalism research concentrates on the producer and practice (public affairs) and cultural studies on the consumer and meaning (private life), and both tend not to dwell on the fact that the practice and meaning of journalism ought to be understood as the same object of study.

In cultural studies, consumers are not conceptualised as passive or behavioural. Like journalists they too are agents - in fact their *sense-making practices* are what make journalism meaningful *as* social uptake. Such practices begin with decoding and may end at the ballot box, the bargain or the barricade. Everyone's position is structural and governed in many ways, but at the same time it is creative, productive and causal; it is *action* not *behaviour*. Here then, in a cultural context, are found *actions constrained by power*, the *making* of sense using classed, raced, gendered and socioeconomically shaped subjectivity within everyday life. So the cultural approach to journalism starts from the 'wrong' end of the value chain. Instead of beginning with origination - the ownership, manufacture or authorship of corporate news - the cultural approach typically starts at its destination, with the readers/audience or consumers of news media, understood as part of culture. From this cultural perspective consumers may be seen as a multimedia 'reading public', successors to the early modern 'republic of letters' (Hartley 2004a; 2004b). They are not reduced to the status of an effect of marketing, media or political campaigning. In the cultural approach, ordinary people's interactions with journalism and news media are investigated within the rhythms and 'personal politics' of everyday life, in order to study the anthropological process of sense-making and identity-formation in modern societies, including cultural struggles and identity politics that frequently don't even rate a mention in mainstream news media, much less in journalism schools.

## Everyone Is a Journalist

The UN Declaration of journalism as a human right is aspirational, a challenge to action rather than a description of facts. It represents an ideal type of liberal democratic polities. If it is to mean anything in practice, it needs to be championed, extended, used and defended. As Aboriginal lawyer Mick Dodson said in reference to the right of Indigenous peoples to self-determination: 'in the world of the real-politic, neither the existence nor even the legal recognition of a right are sufficient to guarantee its enjoyment' (Dodson 1994). Many of the most progressive and important initiatives in journalism since Milton's *Areopagitica* (1644) were undertaken by men and women who claimed journalism as a human right *by practising it.* Without permission, they started to publish journals. From this point of view, journalistic history is an accrual of discourses and practices organised around the simple *exercise* of that right. But there are many forces or powers working to limit the realisation of the UN Declaration, including most of what counts as contemporary journalism, which from this perspective is an *impediment* to its aspirations.

While the professional practice of journalism is historically and politically important, it cannot be used to *define* journalism. For if everyone is a journalist there can be no *theory* of journalism based on its professional production, its industrial organisation (including ownership and control), its textual form (from news to PR) or even its reception, for none of these is essential - they are all real enough, but they are not the generative edge of journalism in a democracy. The *professionalisation* of journalism is, among other things, a restrictive practice designed to create scarcity of labour and therefore work for the already-professionalised.

- The *industrialisation* of media limits those who can communicate on a society-wide basis to the tiny number who can afford the cost of entry into 'mass' media.
- As a *textual system* accrued by custom and practice over several centuries, journalism has taken on some generic characteristics that work powerfully to exclude various forms of expression from what counts as journalism.
- The *regulation* of media is used both correctively and protectively to limit journalism - to redress defamation, obscenity and the like, or to protect identities and minorities from opinions that are legislatively deemed too hideous to be allowed journalistic expression.
- The right to express opinion or to gain information

has been *constrained by power;* in practice it is not neutral as to gender, class, race, age and so on. The 'logic of democratic equivalence' may inspire struggles by various social movements to extend the right to women, workers, people of colour, children and others, but universality is never achieved in practice and even small extensions require struggle and leadership.

Quite a few entrepreneurs have found work and wealth, and some have exercised political or cultural power, by increasing the scale, efficiency and productivity of media communication. Such achievements - even up to the scale of media empires - cannot be excluded from a theory of journalism, but neither can they be its foundation, for the model of journalism that is commercially definitive now can be countermanded by someone having a different idea that catches on, as witness the current ascendancy of personal journalism (blogs) and search-engine journalism (Google News).

## A Writing Public

Opinion and information become journalism only when they are circulated among a public. Media technologies and a literate reading public are both needed to 'impart' them, which is why journalism is a modern phenomenon, unknown in pre-modern societies. Historically, in direct opposition to the UN Declaration, access and even capability have not been generally distributed. While modern mass media, both print and broadcasting, have been very efficient at gathering populations to 'read' on page and screen, such that more or less everyone in the old democracies is at least exposed to journalism, they have been less successful in extending the *practice* of journalism so widely. Modernity has been a 'read only' era for most citizens, not a 'read-write' one. However, consideration of just this problem demonstrates the importance of the UN Declaration because it makes clear that modernity remains an incomplete project, as Habermas has said. Effort is required to extend the practice of journalism to 'everyone'. However, when that is done, or even imagined, the nature of what we habitually understand to be journalism changes completely. Journalism research therefore has to look towards the *history* of ways in which 'everyone' has - or has not - been brought into the public domain of information and opinion, and towards the *culture* in which 'everyone' is located in order to practise their right to communicate. It has to investigate the *uses* of public information and opinion in democratic or democratising societies.

The reading public or republic of letters was one of early journalism's great creations, dating from the age of Johnson, Addison and Tom Paine in the modernising eighteenth century (Hartley 1996; 2004b). It was extended to a mass reading public during the industrialising nineteenth century. For its part, cultural studies was launched by Richard Hoggart's *Uses of Literacy* (1957), a study of the reading public when that public had reached mass scale and the information media had achieved mass entertainment status. Ever since, cultural studies has been preoccupied with the moment at which media production becomes communication and culture - the moment of *use* in the circumstances of ordinary life.

Now the time has come when the idea of a multimedia reading public can be seen for what it really is - a halfway house towards full 'read-write' literacy (Rettberg 2008). The time has come, in short, to think about a *writing public*. Journalism's interest in the democratic process, factual reporting and compelling stories about the real can be combined with cultural studies' interest in critical activism within the context of power, lived experience and ordinary life. Thence it is possible to re-found journalism studies to address the 'writing public'.

## Globalisation and a Redactional Society

A problem yet to be faced here is that, unless a reading public is formed around it, the right to 'impart' information may not be realisable, because in some forms of expression there are more people writing than reading. If everyone is speaking, then who is listening, and on what kind of apparatus? That problem resolves itself into the question of creative editing or 'redaction' - a journalistic practice that is swiftly becoming the defining art-form of the age. I conceptualise contemporary society as 'redactional' (Hartley 2000). The editorial practices of the media, for example, may reveal presuppositions about the culture and the various groups within it, enabling conclusions to be drawn about how meaning is sourced, and explaining differences in the treatment of identities from business leaders and celebrities to foreigners and Indigenous youth. Generalising from such investigations, a 'redactional society' is one in which *editorial* practices determine what is understood to be true and what policies and beliefs should follow from that, and what the contemporary equivalent of beautiful is (e.g. innovative, artistic, sexy, dark, entertaining, cool, original or strange) and how desires should be ordered around that. Such a scenario has emerged out of the combination of late twentieth-century economic and technical ingredients - the globalisation of media and entertainment content and the beginnings of mass scale in the use of interactive communication. Editorial practices are required to make the potentially overwhelming and chaotic possibilities of such plenitude into coherent packages for users, whether these are individuals, businesses or even nations.

This is part of a larger argument about long-term shifts along the 'value chain' of meanings, where what was accepted socially as the source of meaning - and thence legitimacy - has drifted from author (medieval), via text (modern), to consumer (now). In medieval times, the source of meaning was God, the ultimate author(ity). In the modern era, meaning was sourced to the empirical object or document, the observable evidence. But now, meaning is sourced to popular readerships or audiences, and is determined by the plebiscite (see pp. 16-17 above).

In contemporary societies, where values, truths and meanings are fragmented into the number of sovereign citizens or consumers that make up a total population or market, there is no explicit or agreed mechanism (authority) for deciding which should prevail apart from weight of numbers. So elaborate mechanisms have evolved to *scale up* the myriad sources of meaning, and these are proliferating across many areas of public and mediated life. They include *redaction* and *the plebiscite*. Redaction is the art form of editing, where existing materials are brought together into a new form. Journalism has begun to change from news-gathering to a redactional function: a prime job of the journalist is to sift existing data and make sense of that for readers, not to generate new information. The process is evident in Google News, which edits thousands of news websites into one, presenting the top stories around the world via an algorithm (not a journalist but a sort of automated plebiscite) that ranks them by the number of occurrences on the internet and by recency (news value).

Globalisation of digital content consumption also entails a society in which 'everyone is a journalist' or can be. Not only can they express an opinion or circulate information via read-write media forms such as email, blogs, websites, SMS and the like, but their views can be gathered and processed into collective forms, ranging from the question of the day on Sky News to 'best of. . .' competitions run by media organisations like the BBC.

But in the meantime, *journalism* has so massively expanded that it is unrecognisable as *news*. No longer confined to the investigation of wrong-doing in politics, decision-making in government and business, or achievement in sport and entertainment, journalism in non-news areas has rapidly outgrown its parent. Corporate communication, PR and marketing are routinely performed by journalists and as journalism. Fashion, travel, celebrity, makeover and lifestyle shows on TV are among the most envied jobs for aspiring journalists and among the most popular cultural forms. Magazines are more dynamic than newspapers, which have begun to function as magazines, at least on weekends. Information exchange in specialist areas, the traditional province of magazines, has migrated to the web, where there is so much information on any given special interest - genealogy, for instance - that new websites and magazines are spawned to help people navigate it. In short, a society in which everybody is a journalist begins to be imaginable, whether their practice is direct or sampled or mashed-up via some *plebiscitary* or *redactional* representation. This is the terrain that a cultural theory of journalism needs to investigate.

Immediately, questions arise, all of which are good for further research, not least by those who already have a professional interest in journalism:

1. How to **access** the right to write? This involves questions of LITERACY in new media, and not just technical skills but the full array of creative competence that goes beyond *self-expression* to *communication,* and thence to objective *description* and *argumentation,* extending literacy from 'read only' to 'read and write'.
2. How to **organise** and edit the billions of pages of writing? This involves not just technical questions about scaling, data-mining and archiving, but deeper questions about how to edit the pages for a media-saturated population who are producers as well as consumers. These are questions of REDACTION that need to be answered in an 'economy of attention' (Lanham 2006).
3. How to **represent** facts and opinions back to society? This involves questions about how opinions can be scaled up, which are questions of the PLEBISCITE.
4. How to **tell the truth,** and how to tell when it is being *told?* This involves questions of communicational ETHICS.
5. How to **hold together** the 'top' and 'bottom' of a **stratified society?** This involves linking diverse and even conflictual readerships in a truth-seeking discourse about what is happening now. This requires research into the practice of READERSHIP in a context where utterance is valued above understanding (the collective hive over authorised wisdom).
6. How to **evaluate quality?** In an era when *everyone* is a journalist, where are the greats and how do they emerge

into visibility? This raises the question of journalism's appeal and communicability as a textual experience for readers - what used to be called 'LITERARINESS'. What is good journalism, and how can that be *universally* promoted?

If everybody is a *journalist,* then everyone has a right not just to express but also to *circulate* information and opinions that they actually hold, even when these are seen by others as harmful, 'hideous' or wrong-headed (Hargreaves 1999). So-called user-led innovation will reinvent journalism, bringing it closer to the aspirational ideal of a right for everyone. Journalism will be reinvented, but judging by what is currently done in journalism schools and in the name of journalism studies, the last people to know may be professional journalists.

# 7

# Fashion as Consumer Entrepreneurship
## Emergent Risk Culture, Social Network Markets and the Launch of *Vogue* in China
## With Lucy Montgomery[2]

## Waste - or Wealth?

Thorstein Veblen was among the first modern writers to propose an evolutionary theory of economics (Veblen 1899; Carter 2003: 51). He analysed 'honorific' *dress* (that is, fashion) as opposed to 'useful' *clothing* as an illustration of his economic principles. Unlike Marx, he sought the explanation of the economy in consumption, not production, in the systematic patterns of choice, relationship, competition and hierarchy among both the affluent 'leisure class' and all other classes caught up in modern 'associated life'. Dress (as opposed to clothing) evolved historically as the expression of wealth:

> The line of progress during the initial stage of the evolution of apparel was from the simple concept of the adornment of the person by supplementary accessions from without, to the complex

163

concept of an adornment that should render the person pleasing, or of an enviable presence . . . In this latter direction lies what was to evolve into dress . . . What constitutes dress as an economic fact, properly falling within the scope of economic theory, is its function as an index of the wealth of its wearer (Veblen 1964: 65).

If dress is an index of wealth, it requires a system of what Veblen calls 'invidious distinction' or comparison (Carter 2003: 52) and a society-wide means of representation, both dress itself (dress is the 'paper currency' of pecuniary values) and a public medium for circulating fashion signs, for instance fashion magazines. Fashion and fashion media are the means by which status, hierarchy and comparative individual advantage can be socially networked and communicated (Potts et al. 2008). Each individual fashion choice, clothing ensemble and personal 'look' is rich in information that is an expression of both the choices of others in the system (fashion as imitation) and one's own choices (fashion as invidious comparison). Such a system is extremely supple and sophisticated both in range and over time; as Barthes was the first to point out, the meanings communicated through dress are structured like language, and fashion can generate elaborate 'texts' and superfine distinctions. Furthermore, since the entire system is based on individual choices within a system where choices are determined by the choices of others - the very definition of a social network market - it is necessarily a dynamic, changing system, based on novelty. None of these meanings would by itself be strictly economic, but the system itself drives the economy; it is what Richard Lanham has recently called the 'economy of attention' (Lanham 2006).

In *The Origin of Wealth,* Eric Beinhocker (2006) argues

that fashion design is an evolutionary process, involving iterative 'differentiation . . . selection . . . and amplification or scaling up of the successful designs to the next stage of the process', within a social network of designers, clothing companies, retailers and consumers. 'Your shirt was not designed; it was evolved' (14-15). The reason why the fashion industry goes through such a seemingly wasteful process is that its fitness for purpose cannot be predicted:

> The reason that your shirt was evolved rather than designed is that no-one could predict exactly what kind of shirt you would want out of the almost infinite space of possible shirt designs . . . Our intentionality, rationality and creativity do matter as a driving force in the economy, but they matter *as part of a larger evolutionary process* (original emphasis).

The evolution of a garment - a *design* process that nevertheless works by *trial and error* - is only successful if it finds sufficient buyers (or admirers) to justify its manufacture (or mediation). This is coordinated by the market. Here the culmination of the efforts of designer, manufacturer and retailer finally confront the risky moment of choice: the decisive moment.

## Institutions of Learning: The Fashion Media

Neither buyer nor seller goes into the bargaining process 'naked', so to speak. Both parties seek to reduce uncertainty and risk by means of information. The supply side will have used marketing techniques to find out what you are likely to choose, while the consumer has sought information to mitigate personal fashion errors, or to gain a competitive advantage in knowing what's hot at any price, or a bargain at this price. This is not, in other words, a totally asymmetric relationship with all the power in the hands of the seller. Astute consumers may have extensive 'cultural capital' in fashion culture to bring to the experience of shopping, and in intensive, urban environments such capital may be distributed widely among the population, forming a general and often highly developed 'creative literacy' in the meaning of particular choices, combinations and uses.

The forum where such information is shared, where essential learning and feedback are rendered visible, is that of the fashion media, of which the classic form remains the 'glossy' magazine, even though significant innovations have been made in other platforms, for instance fashion advice shows on TV (e.g. Trinny & Susannah's *What Not to Wear; Project Runway*) and fashion websites on the internet. Fashion 'bibles' like *Vogue* have for many decades acted as arbiters of taste: they *represent,* literally and visually, the choices of the fashion-conscious social network.

It is not a foregone conclusion that enough people (choices) will converge on a garment, a designer or a 'look' to justify scaled-up manufacture; and it is by no means certain that a given garment or collection will afford the consumer sufficient novelty and exclusiveness to justify purchase. *Vogue* and its competitors are there to assist in the tricky business of bringing innovation (the fashion value of novelty) into convergence with imitation (the market value of replication), which, despite their opposing logic, are equally essential in any social network market. You want your choices to reflect the highest-status values in the system; this requires emulation of trend-setters, whether they are style entrepreneurs or celebrities. But you want your choice to be unique; this requires constant novelty and innovation to be expressed in the very materiality of your fashion purchases. Fashion media exist at the point of tension between innovation and emulation. They are the mechanisms for learning and feedback by both consumers and producers, and as such are an integral part of the productive process of emergent values (both economic and symbolic). They map the social network that links agents and enterprises in the fashion system, and show agents how to navigate that network in pursuit of individual 'honorific' status choices.

## Fashion and Modernity - Chinese Style

The launch of *Vogue* marks a tipping point in the development of Chinese fashion and fashion media, linking China more closely to the international fashion system, and setting new standards in photography, style and design in Chinese fashion publishing. The launch of *Vogue* China also reflects the growth of fashion and luxury brand consumption in China. It is an important catalyst for the further development of fashion values and consumer culture. The growth of fashion-magazine publishing in China reflects deeper changes that have taken place in Chinese society since Mao's death. Modernisation, economic reform and an 'opening up' to the outside world have been accompanied by the growth of fashion consciousness and fashion values among Chinese consumers. The launch of *Vogue* China might be understood as the 'decisive moment' (in photographer Cartier-Bresson's famous phrase), the moment that readers' desire for fashionable images and information about international style trends converged with advertisers' and fashion-professionals' demands for a reliable, high-quality publication capable of creating a connection with consumers to draw China firmly into the international network of fashion production and consumption.

In spite of the close links between fashion and political culture that are evident historically in China, few researchers have made use of the vast wealth of cultural artefacts, including fashion magazines. As Beverley Hooper (1994a: 164) laments:

> In few societies has clothing been a more significant symbol of a nation's political culture. Yet apart from the occasional reference by western journalists to China's 'blue ants' in the Mao era and to miniskirts and makeup in more recent years, little use has been made of these artefacts.

Michael Dutton (1998) argues that the emergence of Western-style fashion in China is often misinterpreted by outside observers as a sign of a growing sense of individualism and freedom among Chinese consumers. Dutton suggests that, rather than signalling the rise of 'a modern individualised political subject' (275), contemporary consumer fashion culture in China is little more than the recasting of collectivist values in the context of mass production and liberal economic reform:

> In China, especially among the middle-aged, fashion is quite often recoded to promote a collectivist, not individualist, ethos. As though in recognition of the fact that we live in mass-producing and mass-consuming times, many consumers in China do not operate with the notion of individuality that underpins even the most mass-produced of fashion products in the West. For these Chinese,

fashion is not constructed to mark out one's individuality, but
to mark out one's success (275).

In describing the tendency of middle-aged fashion consumers, in particular, to make fashion choices based on
what the majority choose to wear, and to associate 'wise'
choices of clothing with 'popular' choices, Dutton implies
that a particularly Chinese desire to conform persists:

> Success is made verifiable through the notion of correct choice.
> Success means choosing a coat that everyone else is wearing,
> for to see others in the same coat, dress, trousers or shirt is not
> a sign of social disgrace, but a mark of wisdom and affluence.
> One has chosen wisely, for one has made the 'popular choice'.
> In this respect at least, fashion stands in for a wider, deeper and
> more unconscious sense of collective self (275).

Dutton has chosen to discuss the 'fashion statement' in
order to illustrate his point that the most apparently convincing sign of 'Western consumer-individualism' cannot be
taken at face value. Existing Chinese values and habits continue to dominate and economic reform is not necessarily
the 'harbinger of a modern individualised political subject'
(274). However, there is no need for an ethnocentric reading
of this phenomenon, for what Dutton has described very
accurately is not the secret of the Chinese collective psyche
but the workings of the social network market - a process
that can be observed just as readily among consumers and
producers in the West as in China.

A closer reading of the history of fashion in the West suggests that the emergence of fashion values is more complex

than Dutton's comments imply. While it may be difficult to argue that fashion *caused* the social or philosophical shifts responsible for modernity and democracy in Europe, the relationship between what people choose to wear and how they think about themselves and society is well documented (Lipovetsky 1991; Carter 2003; Breward 2000). Indeed, no country has modernised its economy or polity without concomitant changes in costume, or without media to diffuse information and feedback about those changes and their significance. Modernity everywhere was just as much a corporeal experience as an intellectual one. As Gilles Lipovetsky (1991) demonstrates, the rise of a fashion culture is closely linked to deeper changes in society: the predominance of the tastes and opinions of *contemporaries* (rather than traditional authority) in decisions about comportment, and a perception of *change* as a positive force:

> Love of change and the determining influence of contemporaries are the two major principles governing eras of fashion; both entail a devaluing of the ancestral heritage and a tendency to dignify the norms of the social present. Fashion plays such a radical role in history because it institutes an essentially modern social system, freed from the grip of the past (23).

Lipovetsky ascribes causal force not to a 'collectivist ethos' but to its very opposite: 'love of change' and freedom *from* 'the grip of the past'. He allows for the 'determining influence of contemporaries', but does not reduce that determination to any single 'ethos'; as a result, his conceptualisation of the modernising force of fashion is an exact description of the emergence of a social network market.

Li Xiaoping (1998) observes the connection between the modernisation of Chinese society and the emergence of new fashion systems in China. Li argues that the emergence of fashion-consciousness after Mao's death reflected important changes in China's aspirations and a growing sense of connection with the international community:

> Modernization became the major driving force behind the development of new fashion systems in China. In fact, the Chinese term *shizhuang* (fashion) has always signified the modern, as it is clearly contrasted to *fushi* (costume), which refers to clothing styles in Imperial China and of ethnic minorities. It is *shizhuang* (fashion) *not fushi* (costume) that links China to the outside world. *If fushi* always points to tradition and past *shizhuang* is closely associated with internationalization and modernization (75).

According to Li, 'from the very beginning, modernization in China has involved the construction of the "new" or "modern" woman'. Li argues that fashion and popular culture form a major arena of femininity, offering new forms of bodily adornment as well as new role models for Chinese women:

> The re-fashioned 'modern woman' reveals how aesthetic values and body techniques have been reshaped by global consumer capitalism. It also conjures up and adds a new dimension to a historical truth: the female body is now a site on which party politics, consumer capitalism and patriarchy are played out (71).

In an age of modern media and the global circulation of images, the fashion world that China joined was no longer informed only by what one's immediate neighbours or contemporaries were wearing. By 1976 access to models of fashion and lifestyle had become an important part of a global fashion system. With little access to images produced by the fashion industries and popular media elsewhere in the world, China's new fashion producers and consumers had little to work with:

> ... it is clear that in the early 1980s the lexicon of the new Chinese fashion shared little with fashions in the West. Fashion meant brighter colours, moderately altered uniforms that were popular in the 1960s and 1970s, and skirts and dresses modelled on the patterns of the 1950s. After decades of state surveillance over bodily practices, neither state-run garment industries nor private tailors had the experiences and imagination to produce something fresh. Individual experimentation with techniques of selection and combination suggests greater ingenuity in the general climate of post-Mao freedom, yet this was substantially curtailed by the lack of aesthetic and material resources (Li 1998: 75).

'Aesthetic resources' - shared between producers and consumers - are a vital component of a modern fashion industry. They provide consumers with models of fashion and an unfolding image-bank of the current repertoire of choices. They provide producers (designers, manufacturers, retailers) with opportunities to showcase their latest offerings; and they offer aesthetic professionals (photographers, stylists, models) the chance to develop their portfolio and to connect with audiences. Fashion labels use magazines as a theatre in which to convey carefully constructed and fiercely defended images of their brand. Designers, fashion buyers and fashion stylists depend on the fashion media as a source of inspiration and information about what others are making and the images they are creating. As fashion theorist Elizabeth Wilson observes, for consumers, fashion magazines offer entry into 'a magical system':

> Since the late nineteenth century, word and image have increasingly propagated style. Images of desire are constantly in circulation; increasingly it has been the image as well as the artefact that the individual has purchased. Fashion is a magical system, and what we see as we leaf through glossy magazines is 'the look'. Like advertising, women's magazines have moved from the didactic to the hallucinatory. Originally their purpose was informational, but what we see today in both popular journalism and advertising is the mirage of a way of being, and what we engage in is no longer only the relatively simple process of direct imitation, but the less conscious one of identification (quoted in Breward 2000: 29).

Wilson's distinction between the 'didactic' and the 'hallucinatory', 'imitation' and 'identification', or 'artefact' and 'image', is another way of expressing the 'honorific' as opposed to 'utilitarian' value of dress. She sees it as a movement from one side of the equation to the other over time, but it may be more accurate to think of it as a general 'toggle' mechanism between 'substance' and 'style' that characterises the economics of attention (Lanham 2006). The 'magical system' of fashion is made as much of words, images, desires and choices as it is of fabric. It is an elaborate meaning-system within which individual agents and enterprises can associate their individual 'look' with that of others, and differentiate it at the same time.

The development of a market economy in China has

provided a new context for the marketing and consumption of clothing and beauty products (Hooper 1994b), and provided women, in particular, with both the freedom to express themselves through their hair and clothing in new ways and the means to afford the startling array of new items now available to them. In a sophisticated, commercially driven fashion landscape, fashion reflects the aspirations, desires and sensibilities of modern consumers. The choice between different designers or labels allows individuals to identify with the values claimed by brands, capitalising on images created by designers and labels in the construction of their own identity:

> The Modernists, for example, (represented by, say, Jil Sander) are an entirety different breed than the Sex Machines (Tom Ford for Gucci). The Rebels (Alexander McQueen) can easily be distinguished from the Romantics (John Galliano). This is not a question of socio-economic status or age. Members of the Status-symbol tribe (Marc Jacobs for Louis Vuitton) have neither more nor less money than members of the Artistic Avant-Garde (Rei Kawakubo for Commes des Garcons), but they do have very different values and lifestyles (Steele 2000: 7).

The modern fashion industry relies on a common visual and imaginative language. By providing makers and consumers with continuously updated and competitively selected images and concepts that are part of this language, the commercial fashion media play a vital educational role in the formation of a modern fashion industry. The emergence of a domestic fashion media in China is, therefore, an important step in the development of the literacy, skills and sensibilities necessary for China to begin producing and exporting fashion, rather than simply importing and consuming it.

## Vogue in China: Representing Risk Culture

The emergence of a domestic magazine industry since the late 1980s (when *Elle* appeared) has created important opportunities for local editors, stylists, photographers and models. The sector is now crowded and many local titles are not turning a profit, but fashion publishing is an important creative industry in its own right and its growth is providing new opportunities for China's emerging 'creative class'.

In August 2005 *Vogue* launched its much anticipated Chinese edition (Danwei 2005). Comments by Jonathan Newhouse, chairman of the company that publishes *Vogue,* were reported in the media:

> 'The Chinese market is different from anything that's been seen in the world, maybe ever,' says Jonathan Newhouse, chairman of Condé Nast International Ltd, the publisher of *Vogue, GQ, Vanity Fair, House & Garden, Glamour* and *The New Yorker.* Conventional wisdom suggests early arrivals have an advantage. But for *Vogue,* that was not so. *'Vogue* aims at the very top of the market,' says Newhouse. 'So typically *Vogue* is not the first magazine to enter any market. It waits until the market and its consumers have reached a certain level of development' (Zhao 2005).

The same media report (Zhao 2005) quotes Zhang Bohai, director of the Chinese Periodical Association: '"The quality of most Chinese magazines is not satisfactory," he says. "They are under great pressure when more and more international magazines come in the market. So in some way it stimulates domestic magazines to upgrade themselves".' This combination of forces - a lucrative advertising market, consumers at 'a certain level of development' and weak indigenous competition - paved the way for a truly 'decisive moment' when *Vogue* finally hit the streets of China's eastern seaboard cities with the aim of selling 300,000 copies.

For those not familiar with fashion media, the reason for *Vogue's* brand leadership may not be immediately apparent. What does it mean to be the global style 'bible'? What message does this revered text teach and how does it teach it? For one thing, according to editor of *Vogue* China Angelica Cheung, *Vogue* deals exclusively in 'fashion, beauty, art and the fashionable lifestyle' (Cheung 2005: 114). In a highly differentiated market, other titles like *Cosmopolitan* also operate as 'self-help' or pop-therapy manuals for personal problems, sexuality, identity-formation and career anxieties. *Vogue,* on the other hand, represents a contemporary equivalent of the discourse of 'the good life', which spilled out of philosophy and into books about household management and epicurean taste in nineteenth-century Europe and America. *Vogue* offers an 'image' (in Elizabeth Wilson's sense) of the complete woman: its fashion pages are 'portraits of a woman', not a catalogue of clothing; its information, travel and style sections are all variations on the theme of 'good living'. In short, *Vogue* speaks directly to 'honorific' rather than to 'utilitarian' values; these values are located in the social network system of world fashion, rather than being focused on the self-image of the reader.

*Vogue's* love of luxury is of course wasteful in Veblen's sense, but it is far from useless in terms of the overall system of symbolic distinction that drives competitive status within what may be termed a 'risk culture'. Furthermore, it does not require a utilitarian response from readers: it is not a direct spur to consumption ('buy this frock!'), although the commercial value of having garments or brands featured in *Vogue* should not be underestimated. However, the appeal of *Vogue* is not 'material' in this sense. Instead, its utility for readers is to make visible - literally, on the bodies of women in various contexts - the possibilities that govern the image of those who live in conditions of possessive individualist status competition, uncertainty, risk and change. The beauties who blithely strut across *Vogue's* 'Point of View' pages are the personification of risk culture. The reason why a 'certain level of development' is expected among readers is that they need to gain in semiotic as well as economic affluence. The 'astute reader' will understand the play of tension between imitation and innovation; they will see that what is being portrayed is not an instruction to buy but an imagined outcome of the workings of choice.

Fashion itself is *risk culture in action*. Designers and fashion houses (labels) produce novelty and originality season after relentless season. Showbiz types and artists, wealthy families and old-money aristos, who are themselves high-end 'investors' in risk culture, are prominently involved in the industry, in creative and branding positions as well as being iconic or 'apex' consumers. Meanwhile, pressure also comes 'from below' (street fashion, pop-culture, younger models, new designers, photographers and stylists, hot celebrities, the pressure of future choices on present realities if you like) as a form of 'creative destruction' that will renew the system for all players. And the fashion media disperse, to a much wider 'reading public' than those active in the scene itself, the appeal of the restlessness of creative innovation and of emergent knowledge about risk culture. Each fashion spread is 'poetic' (in the original sense of *poïesis:* to make anew); it both transforms and continues the world it represents.

The launch issue of *Vogue* China offered a *convergence* between fashion history, the new look and Chinese readers. In pursuit of that aim, the magazine was careful to visualise a version of the characteristic mode of 'foreign investment' in China: that is, partnership with local players, not sole foreign control. Rather than simply displaying the fruits of world fashion as pure imports, almost every feature tactfully offered a Chinese dimension. Angelica Cheung's editor's letter *(Vogue* China, September 2005: 38) set the tone: it juxtaposed a 1941 photograph taken by Cecil Beaton, showing a woman surveying a war-torn building, with the caption 'fashion is indestructible', with thumbnails of the work of four contemporary Chinese designers featured in the issue. Beaton was well-chosen; a doyen of fashion photography with a fifty-year association with *Vogue,* and a double-Oscar movie career as designer for *My Fair Lady* and *Gigi*, Beaton was also a documentary photographer, one of whose assignments was to create a photographic portrait of war-torn China in 1944 (Beaton 1991). Thus, one of the most legendary figures in Western fashion history turns out to have 'Chinese characteristics'. The message for contemporary readers is clear: China can emerge from a period of fashion destruction to reconnect with fashion's heroic past and to build its own fashion future, represented by Chinese designers Wang Yiyang, Hu Rong, Zhang Da and Wang Wei *(Vogue* China, September 2005: 140-7).

**Vogue China launch cover, featuring Gemma Ward and Du Juan**
*Vogue* China, September 2005, used with permission

Perhaps the most tact was shown in the riskiest place - on the cover, together with the lead fashion set inside. Here *Vogue* solved the sensitive problem of whether to show a Western model or a local one by producing a gatefold cover with no fewer than six models, of whom one was Australian Gemma Ward (the undisputed 'face' of 2005 worldwide) but the other five were Chinese, lead by Du Juan and Wang Wen-qin. These models also featured in the main fashion feature, called 'Shanghai Diary' (282-309). It was styled by the editor of *Vogue* Paris, Carine Roitfeld, and photographed by leading international photographer Patrick Demarchelier. The opening shot shows Ward and Du in identical Prada outfits. Thereafter, Ward dominates the scene, wearing exclusively Western labels and accessories with artful 'Chinese characteristics'. The clothes were structured, wearable, colourful and conservative - even though one was a Galliano confection in pink silk and feathers - with few concessions to impractical fantasy or to the darker side of fashion's appeal. In short, *Vogue* made sure that global fashion values were well represented, while offering new Chinese readers a reasonably straightforward 'diary' approach to visual realisation.

## China in Vogue: Peer-to-Peer Mediation

Once *Vogue* had been successfully launched in China it was time for China to be launched in *Vogue*. Several international editions of the magazine carried articles about the launch itself or featured the Shanghai fashion shoot. *Vogue* Australia, for instance, ran the set as its fashion lead in October 2005, under the heading of 'Eastern Exposure' (183-97): 'Supermodel Gemma Ward takes a cross-cultural joy-ride through the streets of Shanghai as *Vogue* celebrates the season's key looks - from rigorous restraint to opulent volume' (184). Three of the pictures feature Du Juan, who is bizarrely referred to as 'Jennifer'. Here, then, the parochial Australians downplay the significance of China in favour of Australian Gemma Ward's 'supermodel' status.

Not surprisingly, given the role that editor-in-chief Carine Roitfeld played in the Shanghai shoot, *Vogue* Paris paid closer attention. Its October 2005 cover announced a 'Shanghai Special: the new El Dorado and its Creative Heroes' (No. 861, cover), with Gemma Ward and Du Juan posed together for the cover shot. Inside there are several Shanghai-related features, opening with one called 'L'Opium de l'optimisme' (151-2), followed by stories on art in the old industrial area of Shanghai (155-8), on model Du Juan (202), and in both the jewellery and beauty sections (214, 228). Following the fashion pages, there were major features on the rooms of Shanghai creatives, photographed by Hu Yang (262-5), and profiles of various Chinese designers and artists (266-71).

Anchoring it all is the main fashion set, photographed by Demarchelier, designed by Roitfeld, and featuring Ward and Du, as in the launch issue *of Vogue* China. But, interestingly, the set in *Vogue* Paris is quite different from that in *Vogue* China, with not a single image in common. Instead, Roitfeld selected a predominantly white look in the garments (with bursts of red), and most of the photographs are monochrome. A 'documentary' look permeates the set, even though the garments and ensembles are uncompromisingly 'fashion'. Ward is caught in mid-stride, walking purposefully past parked bicycles, wall posters and banners in an old *hutong* district. Another shot shows Du Juan seated in a dark doorway holding a cigarette. We see Ward seated in an interior with hotel slippers on her feet, and again with someone cutting her hair extensions. We also see the two models bound to each other in silk organza as Du holds a coquettish finger-to-the-mouth pose, except that the finger belongs to Ward. Old China and new, documented and refashioned: at once continued and transformed.

The November 2005 issue of British *Vogue* published a diary by Angelica Cheung, the editor of *Vogue* China (Cheung 2005: 113-18). We are shown a picture of five-year-old Cheung, 'proudly holding a copy of Chairman Mao's *Little Red Book*', while she muses that 'in a matter of ten years, Chinese women have made the transition from Karl Marx to Karl Lagerfeld, from Mao suits to Miu Miu' (114). Cheung, who had previously edited *Elle,* records that she 'started on the bottom rung, at an English-language newspaper, and was lucky to be surrounded by (mostly British or Aussie) journalists who alternated between giving me kindly advice and mercilessly winding me up' (114). As far as the content of the magazine went, Cheung had to engage in delicate cross-cultural diplomacy to 'make sure that the all-Western creative team' created a cover that was 'to the taste of the Chinese market'. She told Peter Philips, the make-up artist: 'you guys might think a Chinese woman looks great in a cheongsam, but to modern Chinese women, they remind them of their grandmothers! They want to look like Kate Moss' (118). Cheung had to ask Carine Roitfeld not to dress the Chinese cover-models in black ('bad luck in Chinese culture'), although she did not entirely succeed in weaning her Gallic counterpart off the exotic 'opium' look. However, she was clear that the mission of Vogue went beyond the immediacies of the current season's look:

> There has been some debate about whether China can produce its own top fashion brands and designers. There are a lot of negative voices . . . But I remain positive and this is where *Vogue* comes in. A major breakthrough will lie in the designers' ability to subtly inject Chinese philosophy into very modern designs, as Japanese designers did 20 years ago (118).

Cheung quotes advice given to her by Anna Wintour, legendary editor of US *Vogue:* 'The job of a *Vogue* editor goes beyond the magazine. You should support the fashion industry in your country' (118).

## Entrepreneurial Consumers - Living in Risk Culture

The growth of magazines and the rapid improvement in their content demonstrates the importance of mediating mechanisms in social network markets. These rely on continuous learning and feedback among agents and enterprises alike, if the choices of those in the system are to determine individual choices while at the same time adapting to changed circumstances and emergent values, both economic and cultural. In China their careful but explicit educational function, at least to start with, assists readers to develop an understanding of what is at stake in risk culture. In other words, fashion media like *Vogue* and its newer rivals improve the level of social and economic literacy among a population previously untutored in the semiotics of elaborate choice.

The 'tipping point' represented by the launch of *Vogue* is now past. Since then, *Vogue* itself settled into an evolving dialogue with its own readership, while remaining open to the international fashion system. It is a relatively lonely promontory of *fashion* as opposed to *personal* values, since other magazines retain a high proportion of lifestyle and relationship coverage. To this extent, it may be premature to assert that China has developed a self-sustaining endogenous fashion system. It remains to be seen, for example, how quickly it will develop the dense array of more or less ephemeral avant-garde magazines that characterise global style cities like New York and London. These high-end magazines experiment with fashion itself and with photography, art, design and street culture (not to mention sex and drugs and rock'n'roll). In China, so far only the late Chen Yifei's *Vision* has followed this vein of innovation, often simply by copying international material. Only when such a competitive creative-productive network is indigenised will there be a material basis for internally driven innovation and emergent 'honorific' values. Until then the system is run on international borrowings.

Angelica Cheung is right to heed Anna Wintour's advice to support the country's fashion industry. But support must run deeper than the promotion of local producers and designers. Consumers too - those who would in another context be called 'fans', 'ProAms' or 'apex consumers' (Hutton 2007: 96) - need to be nurtured in their culturally driven, pre-economic creative initiatives, for this is where the 'next best thing' will usually emerge. And a wider readership - a 'reading public' - of fashion media consumers needs to be nurtured, to exert increasingly 'literate' demand-pressure on the system from those with a stake in a social network market for risk culture, creative imagination and consumer entrepreneurship.

Another lesson from fashion is that there are different kinds of innovation. Some industries are changing rapidly as a result of new technologies - the music industry after file-sharing is one. But fashion requires more than technology to drive innovation. It relies on the intense competition of status-differentiation in social networks. New trends are only economically significant if they are copied; but if everyone wears them they are no longer valuable. Hence there is an acute sensitivity to new trends, including those found throughout society and among consumers and amateurs as well as producers and professionals. Fashion is not based on the control of technology to the same extent as other industries; it relies on open complex social networks. It is interesting to observe in this respect that other industries, including those with the major technological affordances characteristic of Web 2.0, are becoming more like fashion.

# 8

# 'The Future Is an Open Future'
## Towards the 'Chinese Century' and Cultural Science

## The Politics of Plenty

In A *Short History of Cultural Studies* (Hartley 2003) I made the claim that cultural studies is a 'philosophy of plenty'; a way of understanding the creation of cultural values among large populations in times of economic growth, democratisation and consumerism. However, these same times - the 'long twentieth century' (Arrighi 1994; Brewer 2004) - were marked by unprecedented social and ideological upheaval, with imperialism, total war, totalitarianism, 'mutually assured destruction' (Cold War) and monopolistic behaviour among corporations as the dark side of progressive secular scientific modernity. Over that long century from the 1880s, world economic and political leadership shifted from European hegemony and British free-trade imperialism to US entrepreneurial-managerial capitalism. The end of the 'long century' was marked by further change, often gathered under the term

185

'globalisation'. For their part, the human, political and economic sciences underwent what has been called the 'cultural turn', associated with post-industrial or network society, the 'new' or knowledge economy, postmodernism . . . and cultural studies.

During that same century, popular culture was characterised by supplementarity of media, where each new medium - live entertainment and spectator sports, the press and publishing, cinema and radio, telecommunications and television, computer games and the internet - supplemented but did not supplant the last, resulting in an overall and accelerating increase in intensity in what consumers did with their time and media dollar. As they found uses for these media, consumers needed to acquire informal but sophisticated multi-literacies; often too they formed themselves into different but overlapping 'discourse publics' (Warner 2002) appropriate to various cultural forms. All these antecedent forms, uses and capabilities are now part of what Henry Jenkins (2006) calls 'convergence culture', where the socially networked user-consumer is the point of intelligibility among competing attractions and distractions.

My argument is that as popular culture passes from 'passive' consumption of representations made by expert others, towards (or further into) active production of direct meanings, experiences and relationships among participatory agents - from 'read only' to 'read and write' modes of communication - it becomes an engine for the further growth of knowledge, driven by self-organising and institutionally coordinated agents and enterprises, who use whatever forms and practices come to hand to achieve self-realisation, to navigate social networks, to seek reliable information and to design authentic experiences.

These are the 'uses' of *open literacies* whose current form happens to be 'digital'. Popular culture is the ground for the growth of knowledge, albeit in undisciplined and multiple forms. In the formal academic domain, cultural studies is an anti-discipline that has proven more sensitive than most to this generative and experimental edge of knowledge.

## Brainchildren of the West

There is no doubt that cultural studies is a Western intellectual enterprise, born out of and seeking to shape specifically Atlantic tensions as economic, political and cultural experience adjusted to American hegemony, carried around the world as much on the wings of popular culture as by military and economic power - that is, by Hollywood, rock and roll, television; everything except sport (whose globalised forms, soccer and the Olympics, are European in origin). Interestingly, it was not during the 1930s to 1950s, the period when American supremacy was established in fact, but later, when it was first seriously challenged - in Vietnam - that cultural studies came to prominence. In the 1960s and early 1970s, popular culture in Europe began to turn the tables on the semiotic superpower by exporting its own music back to it, in the process changing its provenance from black blues to white pop, from authentic expression of oppressed identity to international chart-topping entertainment, albeit through the medium of working-class creative angst and aspiration, embodied in stars like John Lennon of the Beatles and later in the punk explosion associated with the Sex Pistols. Even more remarkable was that musicians began to function as the intellectual leadership of a new generation. It was through commercial music and pop culture that 'countercultural' politics circulated, not through the traditional technologies of democracy and party machines, although the two did collide in noisy ways. This collision happened most notably in the iconic year of 1968 (Gitlin 1993), when Martin Luther King and Robert Kennedy were assassinated as the civil rights movement gained strength, the *evenements* of May set Paris alight, the Democratic Party convention in Chicago dissolved into violence as anti-war activists were attacked by police, students were gunned down in Mexico City, a massive demonstration against the Vietnam War radicalised 'swinging' London (Halloran et al. 1970), the Prague Spring came and went in Czechoslovakia . . . and youth culture turned from dancing to demonstrations:

> You realise that all along
> Something in us going wrong.
> You stop dancing
> (The Who, 1973).

The music-and-drug culture of 'peace and love', the hippie ethic of flower-power, and the 'politics of the personal' arising from feminism and civil rights, merged in 'new social movements' dedicated to the expansion of the mind and to the liberation of women, people of colour, sexual orientation, the Third World, the environment, even children via *The Little Red Schoolbook* (Hansen & Jensen 1971) - in short, the emancipation of culture and identity. These movements were not readily assimilated into the existing labour movement or representative politics, although they did intersect around nuclear disarmament and anti-war activism. Instead they began to create their own media and their own organised forms on *cultural* sites, which were often also commercial enterprises - record labels (the Beatles' Apple), concerts (Woodstock), the 'underground' press, art 'happenings', participatory forms of democracy and a political sensibility formed in *festivals* (culture) rather than in the *factory* (economy) or *forum* (politics).

All of these were Western developments, although countercultural activists were attracted to various revolutionaries from Che Guevara to Mao Zedong, whose works enjoyed a brief vogue among New Left intellectuals, along with those of liberationist thinkers from the Third World such as Frantz Fanon and Julius Nyerere. The question now is whether the passions of the baby-boomer generation created an intellectual system that would outlive their own circumstances; and whether a movement that was essentially internal to the West, struggling against the dominant tendencies of its own social formation, holds any lessons for those beyond that context or born later. Why should, and how can, the ideas and enthusiasms of the 1960s interest non-Western countries like China or young people today?

If history is any guide, there is not much to be gained by seeking to 'apply' Western ideas directly to other contexts, even those ideas regarded as the most positive:

The claim that Western civilization is the bearer of a heritage of liberalism, constitutionalism, human rights, equality, liberty, the rule of law, democracy, free markets, and other similarly attractive ideals . . . rings false to anyone familiar with the Western record in Asia in the so-called age of nation-states. In this long list of ideals, it is hard to find a single one that was not denied in part or full by the leading Western powers of the epoch in their dealings either with the peoples they subjected to direct colonial rule

[India; Indonesia] or with the governments over which they sought to establish suzerainty [China]. And conversely, it is just as hard to find a single one of those ideals that was not upheld by movements of national liberation in their struggle against the Western powers. In upholding these ideals, however, non-Western peoples and governments invariably combined them with ideals derived from their own civilizations in those spheres in which they had little to learn from the West (Arrighi et al. 1996).

In other words, intellectual movements whose origins lie in the West, even those regarded as emancipationist, may be merely a colonising ruse to power if they are imported to the global-South or to the East as part of an attempt to *convert* the locals. They will only be of value if they are propagated as part of a *conversation* in which both parties have a speaking role. Thus, 'applying' the 'philosophy of plenty' directly to current circumstances is simply not going to work. Instead, what is needed is an understanding of what is at stake in the issues, combined with a vigorous effort to investigate the specificities of the new situation from within its own context. In the Chinese case this means avoiding both extremes of 'catch-up' (blind borrowing) and 'get-out' - the exceptionalist alibi, as in the oft-used phrase 'so-and-so . . . with Chinese characteristics' (which tends to turn the thing named, socialism, for instance, on its head). Like other Western ideas, those associated with cultural studies, and more to the point with the problems it has sought to analyse, have assumed global significance in recent years. However, China's own complex history, culture and specific circumstances will necessarily reorder this 'problem situation'. In short, cultural studies is not a method to be applied like a cookie-cutter to all circumstances.

What then is at stake in cultural studies, and how might Chinese and other contemporary readers and researchers make use of its insights for their own forward strategies? Can it be 'abstracted' from its original context and remain useful? Or is it merely a passing trend - less a framework of explanation than a symptom of the times requiring explanation? Such a reflexive question about its own explanatory power is in fact one of the more enduring characteristics of cultural studies, one of its most important moves. Here is a mode of intellectual inquiry that insists on what is called conjunctural (context-specific) analysis rather than scientific universalism, where a problem situation (or problematic) requires its own conceptual framework.

## Cultural Studies and Social Change

Cultural studies was born out of an attempt to understand *social change*. More to the point, it quickly became an intellectual attempt to show how to *provoke* social change in certain areas while *resisting* it in others. In the country and the period in which I grew up, Britain in the 1950s and 1960s, it seemed to some on the Left that, in the place where the Industrial Revolution had begun, decades of activism in the economic sphere (trade unions and the mass labour movement) and in the political sphere (the Labour Party) had not resulted in decisive social change ('revolution') in favour of working-class or progressive interests. However, the Left was also scarred by the events of 1956 in Suez and Hungary, when both Western social democracy and Soviet socialism, in their international guise, were revealed as militaristic coercive forces without emancipationist hope for the locals. Marxism, the favoured 'conceptual framework' for explaining social change, was compromised. Meanwhile, after the home-front egalitarianism of World War II and a short period of state-socialistic nationalisation afterwards (the Labour government of 1945-51), the British working class persistently voted for conservative governments, who presided over a consumer boom, improved housing and employment, and decolonisation too. Some on the New Left thought to ask why, if ordinary people's interests were 'objectively' in line with those of the labour movement, they valued listening to pop music (subcultures) over voting Labour.

Given 'apathy' at home and 'atrocity' abroad, it is no wonder that new sources for progressive social change were sought. Cultural studies has been an extended response to this impasse. The response was both negative and positive. Negatively, those who turned to culture wanted to know if cultural factors were responsible for stopping what had been predicted as inevitable historical change, driven by economic and political determinations. Was there something about culture - in particular the workings of ideology - that needed to be better understood? Positively, it was quite obvious by the 1960s that burgeoning youth culture, subcultures, alternative and countercultures were beginning to provoke social change *through* culture, albeit in its popular commercial forms rather than 'high' culture - in music, performance, film, writing and other arts, which were much more successful at popularising a message or mobilising a community-of-action than anything being done by traditional political parties or workplace agitators (combined). Many on the Left were attracted to the possibilities opened up by these developments, despite the commercial environment in which popular culture thrived. Here, commercial enterprise seemed expansive and communicative, linking a 'we' community. It did not fit the stereotype of an exploitative and manipulative 'they', to which leftist thinking traditionally consigned corporate values.

These things have left their mark on cultural studies to this day. The kernel of the question that remains from this conjuncture is this: what have culture, individual identity and the pursuit of values associated with consumption, leisure and entertainment got to do with social change? A corollary question is: if culture (as well as economics and politics) is implicated in social change, can it be construed as *progressive* (self-realisation; the emancipation of the ordinary) as well as *regressive/repressive* (ideological manipulation by media and corporate interests)? And a third question is: how can the intellectual tools necessary to explain a given situation be understood as part of the object of study? Or, to put it another way, how can social change be understood by its own agents? These very general questions translate well to the Chinese and contemporary context because they remain local questions, requiring specific answers based on contextual and conjunctural evidence.

Furthermore, if it is going to turn out as predicted that China will be the hub around which the next 'long century' is going to emerge into whatever new order is eventually established, then the analytical project of cultural studies has something to offer contemporary inquiry into social change. Its long attention to the 'strategic' relations between *economic* growth/ascendancy, *political* leadership/democratisation and *cultural* experience/identity is worth following. For cultural studies is a very good place to think about how responses to shifts in power are experienced, how individual agency is amplified or stymied by global systems, how creative values

merge or conflict with economic ones, and how the 'performance of the self' may enable or inhibit political change.
As its own economic system matures, China is building a
(demand-led) consumer and services market on top of the
(supply-led) low-cost manufacturing base established in the
first decades of its opening up. To sustain economic growth,
sophisticated, productive, creative agents - both producers
and consumers - are increasingly required. This inevitably
impacts on political arrangements. Growth and development
require individual agency; meanwhile the dynamism of the
system requires spontaneous order (market) rather than central control (decree); and self-realisation for individuals can
occur in conditions that include markets, entertainments and
social networks as well as more traditional political forms.
Cultural studies is an aid to new thought in this area. It was
sparked into life in the first place by an urgent need to understand social change at a moment when existing paradigms of
knowledge, both scientific and political, were in crisis, and
when the drivers of change seemed to be migrating from the
economic and political spheres to the cultural. The need to
understand the role of culture in social change remains in
a globalised world where strategic economic and political
power is shifting from West to East.

## Creative Destruction

Cultural studies has been a disruptive intellectual force in
the West. This too may hold lessons for China, one of which is
that disruptive innovations often provoke quite negative reac-
tions until their widespread adoption and retention neutralise
the 'shock of the new' (in Robert Hughes' famous phrase), when
the progressive and innovative qualities of the disruptive

element can be more clearly appreciated. This certainly has been true for cultural studies as an intellectual enterprise. It has attracted plenty of heat for its tendency to blurt out something about knowledge in general that scientific and policy discourses have tended to ignore or even keep a 'secret' (Birchall 2006). The 'secret' at the heart of knowledge is that *all of it* faces a crisis of legitimacy, because the legitimacy of knowledge cannot be decided in advance. The authority of the author (the expert witness), the adequacy of the method (science), even the apparent obviousness of observation (common sense) - all of these are seen by cultural studies in its 'postmodern' mode as emanating from language, not reality; they are 'constructs', pretexts, ruses to power, or fictions. Cultural studies has attracted sustained derision from scientists (Sokal 2000), from outraged empiricists (it is 'educationally corrupting and professionally embarrassing', Windschuttle 2000), and from those who wish to believe in the truth of the bleeding obvious (journalists).

But, after the heat subsides, it can be seen that this was merely what medical practitioners call 'referred pain'. The *cause* of the problem is not in cultural studies but in modern knowledge itself. Knowledge is now the very engine of economic growth, public policy, business practice and the informed citizen, not to mention the sophisticated consumer, in a 'knowledge economy', 'information society' and 'media culture'. Because of its central importance to all kinds of productivity - economic, political and cultural - knowledge plainly needs to be *trusted.* Equally plainly, it is not trustworthy. Successive crises of legitimacy rock the world, from the question of whether 'big science' is safe (Chernobyl, Bhopal; CM foods; bioscience) and tells the truth (climate change), whether or not a country has weapons of mass destruction (Iraq, Iran), whether politicians *(Independent* 2006), journalists (Danwei 2007) and authors *(Age* 2004) fake their stories, to little local embarrassments for cultural studies itself, notably the Sokal hoax (Sokal 2000).

Cultural studies has had a predilection for 'deconstructive' readings of realist 'texts', not just in the safe playpen of literary fiction but more riskily in the most exposed promontories of the real - that is, science and politics. Small wonder that those with a stake in it express exasperation when 'truth' is undermined. Either it is hopelessly compromised by the uncertainty underlying all knowledge or it is hopelessly pluralised, becoming a property not of *things* but of *experience;* for example when people with religious convictions acknowledge both scientific and divine truths, despite their evident incommensurability. From there it may seem hard to resist a slide to subjectivism where truth means whatever anyone likes, as in TV comedian Stephen Colbert's brilliant concept of 'truthiness' (see Scientificblogging 2008). Despite the protests of those who like their truth to be 'analogue' and straightforward, it can only ever be contingent, mediated and contested. The critics have a tendency to blame the messenger - accusing cultural studies of holding the views it uncovers in texts. They are made even more irritable because cultural studies is often practised at the margins of respectable knowledge, in mass teaching colleges rather than prestigious science departments, or in 'unworthy' subject areas like media, gender or literary studies rather than in medical schools. In other words, cultural studies is seen as a pain in the neck, foisted on unsuspecting undergraduates by postmodern theorists in second-rate universities.

However it is just these symptoms of disruption at the

margins that have led one observer, Richard E. Lee (2003), to claim that cultural studies is part of a much larger crisis of legitimacy of knowledge, one in which it plays the same role for the social sciences and humanities that *complexity studies* have done for the sciences 'proper' (Lee 2004). Together, argues Lee, cultural studies and complexity studies mark 'a shift away from emphasizing equilibrium and certainty', where causality is defined as 'the consistent association of antecedent conditions and subsequent events amenable to experimental replication and hypothesis testing' (Lee 2004). In other words, both cultural and complexity studies have acted as agents of 'creative destruction' (in Joseph Schumpeter's famous phrase) of the modernist paradigm of knowledge, in the natural and social sciences respectively. This is provoking a reordering of the field of knowledge as a whole, in which positivist value-free science and value-laden but economically neutral culture are alike disrupted. Both science and culture have been thrown from Newtonian equilibrium and reinserted into the 'arrow-of-time' of irreversible historical change, which in turn requires attention both to historical contingency and to personal positionality. Lee (1997) writes:

> During the period from the late 1960s, the 'new sciences', emphasizing complexity, irreversibility, and self-organization, have effectively abdicated a role of guarantor of truth in knowledge and reintroduced the arrow-of-time into the natural sciences. The world of nature, like the human world, has now been shown to bring order out of chaos - it is creative; the future is an open future (rather than a predictable Newtonian one), determined only by creative choices and contingent circumstances at unstable moments of transition. This has the effect of freeing knowledge production from the

aporia of uncovering infinite disconnected particulars in search of impossible universals. In a world recognized as creative in all its aspects, values and knowledge, *Wert* [meaning and values] and *Wissen* [systematic knowledge of reality], are necessarily fused.

These far-reaching consequences of early cultural studies were not immediately evident to observers (although they may have been aspired to by some of those involved); but from those small and simple beginnings, seeking to understand how cultural pursuits might trump socioeconomic structures, something of system-wide significance is still propagating, across disciplines, institutions and problematics.

**Excess of Representation; Representation of Excess**

Along the way, cultural studies has been caught up in a crisis not so much of knowledge as of *representation,* which was also entering the period of 'creative destruction' known as postmodernism. Here the legitimacy of both political and semiotic representation, as inherited from nineteenth-century philosophy, was challenged. Commentators became interested in the *productivity of signs,* and in particular the excess of mediation in contemporary societies, whereby signs - often entirely detached from any plausible referent - suffused the public and private domains. Although they were often criticised for turning the world into a text, the postmodernists were among the first to see clearly, right across the domains of politics, culture and the economy, that representation had been emancipated from reality, and that the process of abstracting textuality, signification, meaning and value from situated context or referential causation was a phenomenon of the system, not of their own fantasies. Everywhere, signs were proliferating, and referents retreating. Excessive media signi-fication, in movies, advertisements, TV and the arts, was only the most visible form, easily observed and readily taught. So *media studies* 'caught' postmodernism early and popularised it widely, to the dismay of the nineteenth-century disciplines.

However, *abstraction* and the detachment of the sign characterised even economics, where capital itself was 'tex-tualised' in the form of financial markets, releasing unprec-edented energy into the global financial system. Work was abstracted from the labourer in automated factory systems. The wide distribution of personal computers detached words from pages, allowing 'text' to become mobile in ways that would have astonished typewriter-bashing journalists of the modern era, but they too were busy textualising the world in order to know it. Recipes were abstracted from food, allowing celebrity chefs to prosper even as cooking declined as a social practice. 'The economy' shifted decisively from manufacturing to information. Politics shifted from representative to mediated forms, in which class, party or ethno-territorial loyalty gave way to a system where politicians auctioned promises for votes and events mattered in direct proportion to their visibility on network TV. Culture became the site for the tensions, struggles and 'affordances' associated with these changes to be worked through at the local, contextual and experiential levels.

In such circumstances, which were fully operational in the West just as China began its opening-up process, the most pressing needs were the problems of *plenty* - how to manage information overload, semiotic excess, an *affluence of the mind* that was rapidly extending to whole populations the resources of knowledge hitherto enjoyed only by expert specialists and rich elites. *Productivity* migrated from 'producers' to 'consumers'. The better business plan henceforth was not the one devoted to origination and unique creative invention but the one dedicated to information and knowledge sharing and management - the search engine, the editor, the aggregator, the filter, the synthesiser.

This was part of a more profound shift, where the modernist paradigm of realist representation as a whole was transforming. Excess of representation (postmodernism) was but a symptom of a general shift of productivity (semiotic and economic) further along the 'value chain of meaning'. Productivity is manifested in the assumed *source of meaning* in any system, and this general shift can be observed across many domains and processes (see the figure on pages 16 and 17).

### From DIY to DIWO (Do-It-Yourself to Do-It-with-Others)

Postmodernism was the philosophy of representational excess, but it proved to be a transitional phase, because *representational* and *representative* productivity was soon overtaken by a more *direct* kind, in which consumers began to be producers themselves. This expansion of productivity was closely associated with, and most visible in, the growth of Web 2.0 social networks and DIY applications, although the shift from closed expert system to open innovation network can be observed much more generally, including within the system of political representation (Coleman 2005). While these developments were clearly American in origin and tone - they were individualistic, entrepreneurial, technological and expansionist - their impact was global as the internet followed financial capital and business practices on to the world stage. The consumption of signs, in the form of mass media entertainment supplied by giant corporations (and entrepreneurs with giant aspirations), which had been international if not globalised for many decades, began to feel the heat of competition from the many locally originated user-led innovations (e.g. open source), consumer co-creations (OECD 2007) and DIY cultures (see Hartley 1999: 179-81).

These changes posed a challenge to cultural studies as it had become widely institutionalised, because by this time it had developed a reasonably stable set of concerns about ideology and cultural struggle within everyday life, the politics of the personal, the indeterminacy and reflexivity of knowledge, and a toolbox of methods for demystifying 'dominant' cultural forms and practices. In other words, cultural studies was kitted out to deal with the representational productivity of an essentially industrial system. Now, it is faced with a new kind of productivity - that of the open network, in which individual agency is *creative,* not an effect of power or causal determination from somewhere else (like 'corporate capitalism'). Even system-wide innovations might be seen as 'bottom-up' rather than 'top-down' phenomena, such as 'crowd-sourcing', the blogosphere, social networks, and the reordering of knowledge via 'folksonomy'. The distinctions between expert and amateur, producer and consumer, power and subjectivity, have all been thrown into crisis.

The challenge in these developments is to resist using a cookie-cutter version of cultural studies (e.g. as 'critique') to reduce them to a known framework of analysis before exploring the generative potential of new forms of productivity based on individual agency, technological affordances, global interconnectedness and rapid social change. For instance, a certain branch of 'critique' (see Lovink 2008) has fixed on cultural labour in order to argue that user-led innovation and consumer co-creation are little more than a further step in capitalist exploitation, by normalising casual employment and the 'precarity' of labour, and the dissolution of political activism into consumer commercialism. As always, it is important to maintain critical distance and scepticism in relation to the object of study, but to maintain a *structural* model (of inequality, struggle and antagonism) in the face of *dynamic* disequilibrium (change and growth) is to prejudge how things will turn out, and to deny an open future.

Here then is a fork in the road for cultural studies. It has been well theorised by Mark Gibson, who was among the first to see that the 'career' of cultural studies had taken it on a journey in which its early curiosity about the role of culture in social change had been overtaken by a singular and theoretical concept of power rather than a plural and historical one (Gibson 2002; 2007; see also Cultural Studies Now 2007). Taking one direction at this fork in the road (following Stuart Hall) were those who sought to reduce emergent phenomena to a *structural* model of power. This move recast culture as a zone of conflict (Sinfield 1997 as discussed in Chapter 1; and see Esty 2004: 190; Hartley 2003: 32-7). Power displaced culture as 'whole way of life'. In the 'power' model, especially following the work of Michel Foucault, power was said to be 'everywhere', which led to a tendency for cultural critique to focus on a local, micro-analysis of instances of power, and for it to neglect further macro-scale thought about how the system as a whole might be changing and dynamic, capable of generating 'emergent' as well as 'dominant' values. Thus there is a version of cultural studies that finds power everywhere, but nowhere does it rethink power. Gibson proposes that the concept be pluralised - to 'powers' of various types - and historicised, so that conjunctural analysis can allow for an 'open future', and not an endless repetition of the model. Taking the other fork in the road have been those for whom culture is equated with emergent forms within ordinary associated life, including emergent institutions (the classic forms being the labour movement: trade unions, political parties, and workers' education and welfare associations), but also including creativity, both commercially catered forms and alternative forms. This strand of cultural studies was prominent in media studies, where the tradition of research into active audiences concentrated on the meaningfulness of mass-mediated messages, on the incorporation of audiencing into the routines of everyday life, and eventually led to the study of productive audiences through fan culture and DIY media, a branch of knowledge given a spectacular boost in the burgeoning study of user- and consumer-created content and Web 2.0 applications.

Whether user-created content is critiqued as a corporate ruse or celebrated as an opportunity for 'digital democracy' - whether you see the glass as half-empty or half-full - the fact remains that the rise of self-made media poses important questions for cultural studies. A rethink of the metaphor of 'industry' is in order (see Chapter 2), to get beyond the populist fixation (or intellectualist obsession) with evil capitalist moguls like Rupert Murdoch and Silvio Berlusconi, and to rethink what is meant by production, labour and consumption in terms of complex networks (including markets). This is also to return to cultural studies' real interest in *all* of the agents involved in the system (ordinary life), without opposing them on principle to inherited corporate structures (media industries), institutions that are historically subject to the same dynamic changes as are any other agents. Like the humblest ordinary citizen, the haughtiest global enterprise must adapt or die, as industrial-era media giants have discovered. It is time to abandon the assumption that causation and communication flow one-way only, to recognise causal networks or webs and synchronous causation, and to take seriously the *agency* of the critical-creative citizen-consumer within an overall system in which major enterprises are *also* at work and *also* at risk. This multi-sourced causation in 'scale free' complex systems (Barabasi & Bonabeau 2003), where consumers join in to 'do it with others' (DIWO), is modelled on the 'hubs' and 'nodes' of network theory and complexity studies (Beinhocker 2006; Barabási 2002) rather than on the structural antagonism of Marxian classes.

## Population-wide Creativity as an Enabling 'Social Technology'

This book has argued that the new field of 'creative industries' (Hartley (ed.) 2005) is where this reconnection agenda has been and can be prosecuted most effectively. 'Creativity' (however defined) is generative and emergent (Zittrain 2008); 'industries' (more accurately 'social network markets', see Chapter 2) are the means of society-wide adoption and retention (coordination). Thus the 'creative industries' (the creative economy and culture more generally) are the empirical form taken by *innovation* in advanced knowledge-based economies.

It has been further argued that the general importance of the creative industries far outweighs their scale as a sector of the economy. Their importance extends to their role as a general *enabling social technology,* like the law, science and markets. We rarely assess the importance of the law or science by reference to the scale of the legal or science 'industries'; nor do we measure markets by reference to the cost of maintaining them as markets. It is accepted that such activities enable innovation, growth and human well-being to be sustained across the board. The emergent 'creative industries' - which will eventually have to be renamed to take account of creative economy, creative culture and creative consumers - are taking over in the twenty-first century the position that 'the media' held in the twentieth. However, there is a major difference. In the era of the masses - mass production, mass society and mass communication - the media were conceptualised as the 'social technology' *of ideological control.* But now, in the era of knowledge-based complex systems, the creative industries may be regarded as the social technology of *distributed innovation.* Those who will take forward the study of the growth of knowledge will need to attend to creative destruction of structures and institutions, winner-takes-all innovations, unintended consequences of actions, and sources of productivity well beyond the inherited centres of power (politics), beyond the market mechanism itself (economics), within the sphere of the reproduction of life for whole populations (culture). Such sources include developing countries, teenagers and cultural domains beyond the reach of the panoptic eye of Western modernism to date, even as humanity continues to flock to city life and the attractions of creative culture across the world.

## The Ministry of Enjoyment

The United Nations has announced 'an invisible but momentous milestone' for humanity. In 2007, for the first time in history, we became predominantly an urban species, with

3.3 billion people living in cities rather than in rural areas (UNFPA 2007a). At the same time, 3 billion people - nearly half the total population - are under the age of twenty-five. Around a billion are teenagers, and, of these, nearly a quarter live in China. A 'youth supplement' to the UN report says:

> Young people are often the risk takers and experimenters: they are regularly reminded of their unequal state and lack of opportunities - luxury cars in the streets; smart houses in safe neighbourhoods; opulent lifestyles in the mass media and on the Internet. Exclusion and frustration can lead to crime and violence (UNFPA 2007b, v).

In this quotation is pretty much everything that you need to know to understand why the creative industries are important to the future. Young people are seen as risk-taking experimenters, attracted to the creative 'value-adds' ('luxury . . . smart . . . opulent') of basic services (transport, shelter, communication). The claim is that a billion young people's actions will follow from being 'reminded' about others' success, both physically in the urban environment and technologically through the internet and media. Thus, without knowing it, because the report is clearly more focused on potential failure than on these conditions as drivers of success, the UN report recognises the crucial idea of *social networks,* whereby the actions and choices of young people are determined by the choices of others, in this case those whose previous choices are embedded in affluent lifestyles, both real and symbolic. Youngsters are therefore *agents* in a *social network* system that drives their own risk-taking behaviour, which is the source of entrepreneurship, both creative and destructive.

The UN report goes on to illustrate the human dimension of this scenario with the story of Adegoke Taylor, a qualified engineer who gave up rural life in Nigeria in favour of the uncertain conditions of the city of Lagos, after just one experience of the creative industries:

> In 1999, Taylor came to Lagos. Upon arriving in the city, he went to a club that played *juju* - pop music infused with Yoruba rhythms - and stayed out until two in the morning. 'This experience alone makes me believe I have a new life living now,' he said. 'All the time, you see crowds everywhere. I was motivated by that. In the village, you're not free at all, and whatever you're going to do today you'll do tomorrow.' His future was in Lagos. 'There's no escape, except to make it,' Taylor said (UNFPA 2007a, chapter 1).

This is not to say that the creative industries are infused with the magical power of *juju,* but Taylor's choice of a place to live was based on attraction to a social network (expressed through music, clubs and crowds) rather than immediate economic self-interest. Taylor sought association with creativity and connectivity, valuing these over security and employment. The UN chose to showcase Taylor precisely because he is typical - he represents a global phenomenon and the pressure of the future. And it may be worth adding that one of *juju* music's greatest exponents, King Sunny Ade, is known in Nigeria as the 'Minister of Enjoyment'. He has become 'one of the most powerful people in Nigeria, running multiple companies in several industries . . . He also works with the Musical Copyright Society of Nigeria'.[1] In other words, Taylor's individual experience - enjoying music in a club - is already a successful creative industry, important in terms of economic growth, political influence and law reform, with the power to lure another migrant into *creative competition* (city life), from where 'there is no escape, except to make it'.

So the creative industries are important because they are clustered at the point of attraction for a billion or more young people around the world, and are the generative edge of urban, economic and human growth alike. They are among the drivers of demographic, economic and political change. They start from the individual talent of the creative artist and the individual desire and aspiration of the audience. These are the raw materials for innovation, change and emergent culture, scaled up to form new industries and coordinated into global markets based on social networks.

## Towards an Open Future

The 20th century was the American century; the United States changed the world . . . developing all the major new technologies: telephones, automobiles, television, jet aircraft, the internet and so on. We all assume, as Washington undoubtedly assumes, that we are still living in the era of American hegemony, though it is already clear that China may be an emerging superpower (Rees-Mogg 2005).

Thus, for analysts interested in social change, the creative industries are a bellwether for the 'open future' predicted by Richard E. Lee. Current directions in the study of the continuing encounters among culture, economy and politics do not focus so much on struggle, subject-positioning or structure, as on change, disequilibrium and growth. It does seem to

many that the current period is one of indeterminacy between two relatively stable 'long centuries' - the existing
'American' one and the coming 'Chinese' one (Shenkar
2004; Fishman 2004; Rees-Mogg 2005). Therefore, contemporary readers and researchers who are interested in the
evolving conceptual framework gathered under the rubric of
'cultural studies' need to look out for the next stage, when
'disruptive renewal' stabilises into a new emergent order.
At that point - which is now - we should strive to develop a
'macro' model of the overall dynamic knowledge system in
which cultural, economic and political values can be studied
in a unified way. If emergent creative innovation is itself an
'enabling social technology', then analysts will need to focus
on local-global instances of *popular creativity,* the *productivity of consumption,* and the propagation (especially via the
internet and other technologically enabled social networks)
of the *means of semiotic production* across whole populations, coordinated in hybrid social network markets that allow
commercial and community enterprises, markets and selves,
corporate giants and micro-businesses, to coexist and co-create
values. In such a context it will be possible to understand the
uses of creative and cultural resources - open digital literacies
- for enterprise at both the community and the commercial
level, and to extend from 'defensive' cultural identity to
expansive, mobile and distributed creative innovation.

In this context cultural studies emerges not only as a
philosophy of plenty but also as a resource for policy and
practice: it can become a useful conceptual framework for analysing innovation systems, creative industries, enabling social
technologies, the propagation of creative productivity and the
growth of knowledge across whole populations. To do this,

it will have to shift its centre of gravity from West/North to East/South, in order to understand and accommodate the further extension of popular digital literacy into non-canonical but productive domains - including Mandarin and the other growth-languages of global intercourse. And it may have to change its name as well - to 'cultural science'.

## Towards Cultural Science (Once Again)

The main thing holding cultural studies back at the moment is the limited ambition, amounting sometimes to defeatism, of its own practitioners, who excel at in-close 'micro' analysis of local specificities without reaching for an adequate 'macro' level of conceptualisation to replace the long-dominant but now abandoned Marxist framework. Given the incredible energy and productivity of popular culture itself, this failure to develop a concerted strategy of theory-formation and conceptual framework development, to understand how new media, popular sense-making and global commercial enterprise are affecting the growth of knowledge, is damaging. Cultural studies needs to move beyond endless case studies based on a few dozen texts or respondents that are designed to show the exceptionalism of local instances rather than the dynamics of the system as a whole (a bad habit for which it was criticised many years ago by Meaghan Morris, 1990). Equally, cultural studies needs to avoid the thoroughly criticised temptation to universalise from such particulars. Projecting the fears, desires and cultural prejudices of the analyst onto the object of study is a bad old habit of both literary critics and imperialist science that cultural studies has resisted from the start. However, the productivity of popular culture - of open digital literacy among non-specialist agents and enterprises - is now such that it demands a more systematic response than can be achieved by maintaining a 'struggle' stance; pushing at the police line, as it were (and as discussed in Chapter 1), without a purposeful objective beyond enjoying the experience with like-minded others.

The failure to think systematically seems to result in part from the capture of cultural studies by 'culture wars' partisanship, where ideologies and values have become more important than description and theorisation. Such partisanship is quite understandable when 'neo-cons' stalk the corridors of power and the airwaves, in Washington at least, but it makes for poor science. Cultural studies has become most strongly established at the 'values' end of the disciplinary spectrum, the polar opposite of the quantitative sciences. It is becoming the secular successor of that branch of clerical training concerned with sermonising - using rhetoric, textual exegesis and moral precepts to guide the young in public values, personal comportment and a vision of ethical living. This is of course valuable and useful, but it is a long way from science; even as modified by the 'creative destruction' of complexity and cultural studies, and even if the most progressive definitions are used, for instance that the word 'science' describes 'contested knowledge'. In cultural studies, we have too much contestation and not enough knowledge. It is hard to contribute to the process of self-correcting knowledge (another good definition of science) without engaging in it directly, that is, by self-correcting the knowledge domain of cultural studies itself.

Strangely enough, this is exactly where cultural studies came in. Richard Hoggart himself saw the need for his own field - modernist literary criticism - to engage with the social sciences; this was his project in the early days of the Centre for Contemporary Cultural Studies (CCCS). He sought the input of sociologist Alan Shuttleworth, who presented a paper on 'Max Weber and the "Cultural Sciences'" (Shuttleworth 1966). This theme was later picked up by that other pioneer of cultural studies, Raymond Williams. In 1973 he made a speech to the Council for National Academic Awards (CNAA), the body charged with the modernisation of the higher education curriculum in the United Kingdom via the new Polytechnics, whose degree schemes were validated by the CNAA.[2] Williams used the occasion to propose something new - a risky enterprise, as he knew only too well from working in the 'old' humanities:

> You can go on doing, in effect without challenge, virtually anything that has ever been done, but if you propose anything new you are lucky if your integrity escapes whipping; your intelligence and sensibility will have been long given up as dead (Williams 1974).

Undaunted, Williams went on: 'The approach I want to describe is that of cultural studies, which is English for "cultural science".' Williams traced the study of culture from early modern attempts to understand it as general human development driven by spirit or consciousness, to the Marxist notion of culture as material production. He wanted to move on, to identify the 'central problem' of cultural science as 'the relations between different practices', and thence to see communication itself as a practice amenable to analysis by cultural science. He borrowed the term from continental sociology after Weber and Dilthey. It is worth noting here that the binary split between arts and sciences that bedevils Anglophone disciplines is unknown in continental ones, where the 'human sciences' are part of science, because science refers to knowledge in general, not only to white-coat experimentation. Williams was attracted to the *openness* of 'cultural science' and this is what he wanted to translate into English as 'cultural studies':

> Out of this argument, about the relation between practices, came the new concept of cultural science and with it a significant part of modern sociology . . . Now the spirit of this whole inquiry - to which literally thousands of people have contributed - is profoundly open, alert, and general. It has had its bitter and even its squalid controversies, and this is understandable; but in temper and approach it is in a wholly different dimension from what seems our own small world of small cultivators, heads down to their own fields . . .
>
> I recall the spirit of cultural science because I am interested in its heirs - who will change its methods but will still inherit its vigorous and general humanity . . . The work will be done because I think there are now enough of us who want to work in these ways . . . to announce in effect an open conspiracy: that in new ways, by trial and error but always openly and publicly, we shall do this work because it needs to be done (Williams 1974).

An 'open conspiracy' among those 'thousands of people' and their heirs who, systematically in theory but by trial and error in practice, and in a spirit of 'vigorous and general humanity', seek to study the *relations between different practices:* this is the prolegomena for cultural science still, even though the project itself has been updated and refined to study *evolutionary change* in practices, and not just their *structural relations;*

as for instance in this 'provisional statement for cultural science', in which I had a hand:

*A provisional mission statement for cultural science:*

- Creative productivity has always emerged from human inter-actions, but it is increasingly mediated by technologies that promote subjective mental representations as networks, in which space and time are compressed through the continual dissemination and retrieval of stored events.
- The interaction of people within this 'social network economy' creates a continual flux of ephemeral communities and novel entrepreneurial opportunities, with unforeseen consequences being the norm rather than the exception.
- This process of 'creative destruction' is best addressed by the humanities allying with the dynamic science of evolution - the study of continual change through variation, interaction, selection and drift.
- Cultural science therefore seeks an evolutionary understanding of a knowledge-based society past and present, in order to map the possibility space of future scenarios for creative productivity (both market-based and in community contexts) to which public policy and business strategies must adapt (<cultural-science.org/>).

The need for cultural studies to return to its cultural-science roots is the more urgent because it risks being overtaken, displaced and supplanted. A long-term trend can be observed in which disciplines once located in the humanities have drifted ever more firmly into the mathematical sciences - biology (once 'natural history'), geography, economics and psychology to name a few. Some of these, especially psychology and neuroscience, are becoming ever more confident about explaining culture. So too are the evolutionary sciences: game theory, complexity theory and evolutionary theory. Indeed, it is evolution - the adaptation of complex dynamic systems to change - that can bring the humanities and sciences back together - in particular, evolutionary economics, cultural studies and the creative industries. The cutting-edge of research on creativity lies in the triangulation of three domains: evolution, complexity and creative innovation. This interdisciplinary interface is counterintuitive but highly productive:

- Creativity can be understood as reflexive adaptation to unpredictable change within complex systems.
- Complexity studies explain how social network markets are a vital enabling technology for the distribution of choice.
- Evolutionary theory focuses on the dynamics of change in the growth of knowledge.

Cultural science identifies patterns of action in complex social networks: their past evolution and possible future scenarios, including paying attention to unintended consequences of choices at any given moment. Some of that work must involve mathematical modelling, computational research power, large-scale data-collection and much greater attention to robust empirical methodology than has been evident to date. All of these developments can assist those coming from the humanities, including cultural studies, ethnography and the creative arts, to rethink creativity as a property of agency in dynamic systems. But there will be pain for some: practitioners of cultural science must engage with another kind of digital literacy - mathematics. As the pioneer of artificial intelligence John McCarthy says, 'He who refuses to do arithmetic is doomed to talk nonsense.'[3] Harsh! - but increasingly true, even for those who work in the humanities.

Reflexive creativity is what enables human culture to adapt and change, a process that - despite some 'mass extinctions' throughout the millennia - has resulted in an exponential growth in knowledge and in the creation of new values, both economic and cultural. Culture can no longer be seen as the preserve of artists. It is made up of the activities and productivity of the millions who interact in the social networks that are now dispersed among whole populations. With the growing ubiquity of digital media these are becoming a more dynamic source of productivity than industrial innovation, and it is here that we will find the most important 'uses of digital media'. The social network 'swarm' outperforms the IP-protected 'lab', and at twice the speed. One of the best examples of how that sort of innovation works is in science itself; astronomers and physicists use digital networks to increase the scale and speed of their calculations. But the same model works in fashion, where constant innovation is equally imperative and a complex social network market determines individual choices in a culture that relishes risk. Such systems can be analysed using both in-close contextual techniques from the humanities and computational power to map social networks of choice and change in the way that people perform their cultural identity and relationships (themselves and with others), a process that is well under way in internet and network studies. Theory-building is also vital to model how such actions are patterned in complex adaptive systems, and how agents and enterprises navigate those systems.

What does this mean for digital literacy - and its uses? We are modelling individual creative innovation, which cannot be practised without digital literacy, as part of a large-scale, population-wide process - the growth of knowledge - analysed at a macro or system level. Some of the most important problems in this context are clustered around participation, of both agents and enterprises, in a context where industrial-age expertise competes with population-wide access and use. From this perspective the creative industries and new digital media can be seen as a kind of 'creative wrecking ball' or experimental lab in relation to existing models of both economic growth and cultural participation. We are convinced that the 'creative destruction' of some well-established knowledge paradigms is overdue in both economic and cultural analysis; and should form an important focus for research, both empirical and theory-forming, over the coming years. Some challenging ideas are already in play, for instance the Santa Fe Institute's attempts to produce a computational science of society.[4] We hope to establish principles and directions for future research in the field of cultural and economic values, leading to a new cultural science. The empirical focus is on the shift from closed expert process (professional production in vertically integrated firms) and structural analysis to an open innovation system and complex adaptive networks, for example investigating social network markets. The fundamental problem to be addressed is how knowledge is evolving in a dynamic and complex open system that unifies the economic and cultural spheres and harnesses the energy of all the agents in the system, both individuals and enterprises. That is what digital literacy is *for*, even if that is not yet its principal 'use'.

# Notes

## Chapter 1: Repurposing Literacy

1. For what fag means in this context, see <en.wikipedia.org/wiki/Fagging>
2. 'Q' was the pen-name of Sir Arthur Quiller-Couch, Cornish author, critic, first professor of English at Cambridge and prime anthologist of English literature *(The Oxford Book of English Verse)*.
3. The remainder of this chapter is adapted from A *Creative Workforce for a Smart State: Professional Development for Teachers in an Era of Innovation,* which I drafted for the Queensland government's Ministerial Committee for Educational Renewal (MACER) in March 2004. (The full report is accessible at <education.qld.gov.au/publication/production/reports/pdfs/creativewforce.pdf>.)

## Chapter 2: From the Consciousness Industry to the Creative Industries

1. See <www.google.com/corporate/tenthings.html>.
2. This news item appeared days after Chernin was reported to have earned $34 million that financial year - more than his boss, Rupert Murdoch. See <www.guardian.co.uk/media/2007/sep/07/citynews.business>.
3. See <johnaugust.com/glossary>.
4. 'Spare money' is George Bernard Shaw's gloss on 'capital'. He claimed to have taken the term from the economist W.S. Jevons (Shaw 1937: 463).
5. See Davies' obituary: <www.guardian.co.uk/Archive/Article/0,4273, 4024597,00.html>.
6. Choice includes recognising weakness and loss in a transaction that nevertheless results in a gain for the weaker party. For instance, academic authors often choose (are obliged) to sign over copyright in their work to a publisher in order to get published. They relinquish rights to gain readers.
7. See <www.culture.gov.uk/3084.aspx>.
8. Source: <www.hm-treasuiy.gov.uk/budget/budget_06/biid_bud06_speech.cfm>.
9. See <www.iipa.com/pdf/IIPA2006CopyrightIndustriesReportPress ReleaseFINAL01292007.pdf>.

10. Source: <www.culture.gov.uk/4848.aspx>.
11. Source:<www.industry.qld.gov.au/dsdweb/v4/apps/web/content. cfm7id=6738>.
12. The CCI's (ARC Centre of Excellence for Creative Industries and Innovation's) 'creative trident' is a method for calculating employment in the creative industries by counting three components: 'core' creative workers, 'support' occupations in the creative sector, and creative occupations 'embedded' in other types of firm (Higgs et al. 2008).
13. Its 'provider' perspective leads NESTA to advocate a stronger IP regime, which is antithetical to the 'sharing knowledge' priorities of user-led innovation (NESTA 2006: 41).
14. See<www.culture.gov.uk/reference_library/rninister_speeches/2097. aspx>.
15. Quotation found at <www.culture.gov.uk/what_we_do/Creative_ industries/creative_economy_programme.htm>, accessed February 2008. Page since removed, but see also <www.culture.gov.uk/images/ publications/CEPFeb2008.pdf> *(Creative Britain* strategy document, 2008) where the 'creative hub' is even more encircling, and <www.cep. culture.gov.uk/index.cfm?fuseaction=main.viewBlogEntry&intMT EntryID=3104> (creative economy data).
16. Journalist-blogger Jay Rosen coined the phrase 'the people formerly known as the audience'; see <journalism.nyu.edu/pubzone/weblogs/ pressthink/2006/06/27/ppl_frmr.html>.
17. Wikipedia is good for this word; or check Comedy Central: <www. comedycentral.com/sitewide/media_player/play.jhtml?itemId= 24039> see also Scientificblogging (2008).
18. See <setiathome.berkeley.edu/; worldwithoutoil.org/>.

**Chapter 3: Bardic Television**
1.   David William Nash was an early debunker of the mystic (druidic and shamanistic) claims of Celtic revivalism, such as those associated with lolo Morgannwg, which are, however, still popular in new-age circles (Matthews 2002). Instead, Nash argued for historical and contextual analysis, and for accurate translation (Nash 1858). His work founds the argument seeking to be advanced here, that bards were a regulated part of medieval society, with an institutionalised cultural function that - allowing for technological change - persists. See also Ford (1992) and Guest (1849).
2.   'Taliesin' remains a viable brand-name to this day. Among other things it is the name of a prominent Welsh journal, an arts centre in

Swansea, and various private companies, not to mention its second life in architecture as the name of Frank Lloyd Wright's home. In the way of these things, 'bardic function' is also becoming a brand, emancipated from its origins, as for instance this eponymous blog: <eekbeat.blogspot.com/>.

3.  For the regulation of gifts and 'vagabond' minstrels, see Nash 1858: 33, 179; Morris 1889: 12-13); see also <www.llgc.org.uk/?id= lawsofhyweldda>.

4.  'In Homer, the term *geras* means a "prize of honor, an honorific portion" ... Solon's use of the term *geras* shows that he ... conceives of this due recognition as a part of the distributive fairness that he tries to institute in settling Athenian strife' (Balot 2001: 87-8).

5.  See <cy.wikipedia.org/wiki/Categori:Barddoniaeth_Gymraeg>.

6.  A contemporary account (accessible at <llandeilo.org/rhys_ap_gruffudd. php>) describes the first recorded eisteddfod, showing its characteristic elements of open competition, 'public' or 'state' sponsorship, and the mixture of musical and verbal arts, thus:

    1176-And the Lord Rhys [ap Gruffudd] held a grand festival at the castle of Aberteifi [i.e. Cardigan Castle] wherein he appointed two sorts of contention; one between the bards and poets, and the other between the harpers, fiddlers, pipers and various performers of instrumental music; and he assigned two chairs for the victors in the contentions; and these he enriched with vast gifts. A young man of his own court, son of Cibon the fiddler, obtained the victory in instrumental song; and the men of Gwynedd obtained the victory in vocal song [i.e. bardic poetry]; and all the other minstrels obtained from the Lord Rhys as much as they asked for, so that there was no one excluded. And that festival was proclaimed a year before it was held, throughout Wales and England and Prydyn and Ireland and many other countries. (From the entry for 1176 in *Brut y Tywysgogion [The Chronicle of the Princes],* published in 1860 by the Lords Commissioners of Her Majesty's Treasury under the direction of the Master of the Rolls. Reproduced in Allday 1981: Appendix IV, this quotation 174)

7.  Griffith (1950: 141) writes of pre-modern eisteddfodau: 'The meet ings of the bards . . . were not held for the purposes of entertaining an audience, nor for the production of literature: they were sessions of professionals for the study of the rules of Welsh prosody, and to let performance establish the headship of the profession and the degrees of qualifications.'

8.  For South Africa, see <www.sowetan.co.za/article.aspx?id=466044> (SA School Choral Eisteddfod). For Australia, see Lees 2008 and:
    *   <www.eisteddfod.org.au/aesa/history.html> (Association of Eisteddfod Societies of Australia)
    *   <www.queenslandeisteddfod.org.au/content/view/3/l/> (Eisteddfod Society of Queensland)
    *   <www.nationaleisteddfod.org.au/> (Australian National Eisteddford).
    Among the main Welsh eisteddfodau, apart from the thousands in schools and community centres, are:
    *   Eisteddfod Genedlaethol (the National: <www.eisteddfod.org.uk/english/>)
    *   Urdd Gobaith Cymru/Welsh League of Youth (<www.urdd.org/eisteddfod/?lng=en>)
    *   International Musical Eisteddfod at Llangollen (<www.international-eisteddfod.co.uk/>).
9.  For Bryn Terfel's biography, see <www.musicianguide.com/biographies/1608002839/Bryn-Terfel.html>.
10. See <www.rockchallenge.com.au/modules.php?op=modload&name=PagEd&file=index&topictoview=l>.
11. See <www.rockchallenge.jp/>.
12. Extracts from the Japan Rock Challenge's 'Creating a Theme' are taken from <www.globalrockchallenge.com/jp/modules/PagEd/media/creatingatheme_eng.pdf>.

## Chapter 4: Uses of YouTube

1.  Chief investigators on YIRN were John Hartley and Greg Hearn; researchers were Jo Tacchi and Tanya Notley. YIRN was funded as an ARC Linkage project with Arts Queensland, Brisbane City Council, Queensland Office of Youth Affairs and Music Queensland as partners (Hartley et al. 2003).
2.  Most Australian states ban school use of YouTube to resist 'cyber-bullying': see <www.australianit.news.com.au/story/0,24897,21330109-15306,00.html>. For an interesting discussion of the pedagogy of banning internet affordances in university teaching, see <www.theargus.co.uk/news/generalnews/display.var. 1961862.0.lecturer_bans_students_from_using_google_and_wikipedia.php>.
3.  See <youtube.com/watch?v=-_CSolgOd48>.

4. See <youtube.com/user/lonelygirl15>; see also the entry in Wikipedia, which claims over 70 million combined views for LG15 on various platforms (September 2007), including YouTube, Revver, metacafe, Live Video, Veoh, Bebo and MySpace.
5. See <youtube.com/watch?v=16z60GWzbkA>.
6. Some cultural scientists dispute Barabasi's concept of preferential attachment, preferring a model of random copying. See Bentley & Shennan 2005. YouTube may be a 'live experiment' to test these different explanations for how social networks evolve.
7. For the full speech on YouTube, see <youtube.com/watch?v=faMTYP YfDSE&feature=related>; and <youtube.com/watch?v=Oz9RIjG WpJk&feature=related> (the section quoted is on the second clip). See also <www.whitehouse.gov/news/releases/2003/05/20030501-15.html>.
8. Searching 'mission accomplished' on YouTube yielded nearly 900 videos (April 2008). See, for instance, <youtube.com/watch?v= GJUGUYsm68> (ABC News story previewing the speech); and <youtube.com/watch?v=1lfjmr-Kmxk&feature=related> (re-versioned footage from USS *Lincoln*).
9. See also Michiko Kakutani (2005), 'The plot thins, or are no stories new?', *New York Times*, 15 April, accessible at <www.nytimes.com/2005/04/15/books/15book.html>.
10. See <en.wikipedia.org/wiki/Maslow's_hierarchy_of_needs> (Maslow); and <en.wikipedia.org/wiki/Analytical_psychology> (Jung).
11. Adapted from a good account of Booker's ideas by Chris Bateman at his blog *Only a Game:* <onlyagame.typepad.com/only_a_game/2005/10/the_seven_basic.html>.
12. The British media regulator, Ofcom, has a statutory duty to promote media literacy among the UK population. Its definition of media literacy was arrived at after extensive consultation: 'Media literacy is the ability to access, understand and create communications in a variety of contexts.' See <www.ofcom.org.uk/consult/condocs/strategymedialit/ml_statement/>; and for the full range of Ofcom's media literacy reports, see <www.ofcom.org.uk/advice/media_literacy/medlitpub/medlitpubrss/>.

## Chapter 5: Digital Storytelling

1. QUT's work on digital storytelling has been distributed, iterative, collaborative and conversational, and thanks are due to many col-

leagues, especially Jean Burgess, Helen Klaebe, Kelly McWilliam, Angelina Russo, Jo Tacchi and Jerry Watkins.

2.  In the spirit of participation, I am a digital storytelling practitioner, having made *Perfect Rock* (2004) in a QUT-run workshop, and co-created (with Sandra Contreras and Megan Jennaway) *Brisbane's Best Tree* (2005) in a masterclass run by Daniel Meadows.

3.  'Digital storytelling - Critical accounts of a Californian export' (organiser: Knut Lundby), pre-conference of the International Communication Association Annual Conference, 24 May 2007. A further panel at the 2008 conference was chaired by ICA president Sonia Livingstone.

4.  Namely, overcoming the monster, rags to riches, the quest, voyage and return, comedy, tragedy and rebirth (Booker 2004). See Chapter 4; see also <www.telegraph.co.uk/arts/main.jhtml?xml=/arts/2004/1 1/21/boboo21.xml>: 'There may be only seven basic plots, but there are thousands of stories. What we call the greatest of these are works that stand out from the crowd, and their greatest readers are those who give due weight to each one's own peculiarity.'

5.  Phrase attributed to Richard E. Grant (<www.imdb.com/name/nm0001290/bio>).

6.  See <www.panslabyrinth.com/>.

7.  See his own version of the story at <www.commedia.org.uk/about-cma/cma-events/cma-festival-and-agm-2006/speeches/daniel-meadows-speech/>.

8.  'Mae DS2 yn anelu at ysbrydoli, annog a dangos i chi bosibiliadau cyffrous y maes Adrodd Straeon Digidol *os ydych yn gweithio mewn addysg, y gymuned neu fel artist*' (<www.aberystwythartsceiitre.co.uk/information/Digitalstorytelling.shtml>); author's emphasis.

9.  For example, Best New Media at BAFTA Cymru, 2003.

10. See <www.youtube.com/watch?v=RSHziqJWYcM>, and Wikipedia.

11. See <www.bbc.co.uk/wales/capturewales/about/>.

12. See Derek Malcolm on Robert Flaherty's *Nanook of the North:* <film.guardian.co.uk/CenturyJDf_Films/Story/0,,160535,OO.html>.

13. *Night Mail* is Griersonian rather than by Grierson himself; see <www.screenonline.org.uk/filrn/id/530415/index.html>; and on the problems of expertise in documentary, see the chapter on *Housing Problems* in Hartley 1999:92-111.

14. For example, Frederick Wiseman's *Titicut Follies* (1967); on this, see Miller 1998.

15. See <www.imdb.com/tifJe/tt0139612/>.
16. The film itself is available at <www.moviemail-online.co.uk/films/9186>.
17. See<www.amazon.com/Waiting-Fidel-Michael-Rubbo/dp/B0002XLlP8>.
18. See <www.imdb.com/name/nm0747808/>.
19. <www.allaboutolive.com.au>.
20. Olive Riley (aged 107), on seeing her portrait: see <www.allaboutolive.com.au>. See <www.smh.com.au/news/web/seniors-circuit/2007/05/16/1178995169216.html?page=2> (news story on Olive, Rubbo and the blog from the *Sydney Morning Herald*); <abc.net.au/tv/guide/netw/200602/programs/ZY7518AOO1D13022006T213 500.htm> (Rubbo's film); and <www.abc.net.au/westqld/stories/sl881943.htm> (feature on ABC Western Queensland about the blog, with a call for photo-contributions). Olive Riley died on 12 July 2008, aged 108; see <www.allaboutolive.com.au/2008/07/21/olives-funeral-and-what-id-prepared/>.
21. Rubbo replied to almost every comment on the blog. The following exchange explains his relationship with the technology (note that the comment is addressed to Olive but Rubbo replies in his own voice):

'May 18th, 2007 at 2:06 am *Liisa Rohumaa* says: Dear Olive, I, too, am an admirer of your blog! I would love to hear your thoughts on why more older people don't blog. (I am doing an MA at Bournemouth University and doing some research on 'silver surfers' and the web.) Regards, Liisa

Hi, *Liisa. I am thinking about your question ever since one of our readers in the US discovered how old I am, and expressed surprise that I'm so plugged in to blogging. Actually, I'm still very much at my limits everyday but somehow have overcome fear of the computer and its manipulation. It's very much a mind set I think. Once I decided that it was do-able and I would learn, it began to be a lot easier.*

*Knowing Eric Shade, who's the world's oldest electronic journalist most probably at 87, has helped. But Eric professes not to be able to do what I can now do, and has an 'I can't go much further' attitude. I think he'll probably change that.*

*I very much enjoy being able to take a photo for instance and know that with a few steps, I can get it (1) out of the camera, (2) saved into My photos, (3) into photoshop for cropping and color balancing, and then soon afterwards, (4) into a new post on the blog.*

*But ask me how to wrap text around that same photo, instead of just having text and photo alternating as I now do, and I'm lost again.*

*Going that extra step seems as mysterious and remote as did the things I now know so well. But, of course the difference is that now I think, 'well, that must be easy too actually, just a matter of further learning like before.'*

*The worst experience is something going wrong, not knowing why and losing loads of confidence in the whole business. But that is happening less and less these days. I seem to be more tuned to the computer's moods and vagaries. Mike the helper.*

### Chapter 6: A Writing Public

1. See <www.drudgereport.com/>.

### Chapter 7: Fashion as Consumer Entrepreneurship

1. This is a published rewording of an interview quip: 'I tell people what they want to hear, then I do what I want', the implication being that there is causal sequence in these two actions.
2. Lucy Montgomery is a postdoctoral fellow on the ARC Federation Fellowshipprogram, *The Uses of Multimedia*, at QUT.

### Chapter 8: 'The Future Is an Open Future'

1. See Wikipedia: <en.wikipedia.org/wiki/King_Sunny_Ade>; and see <www.afropop.org/explore/style_info/ID/18/juju/>.
2. The CNAA validated Britain's first degree courses in communication studies - first at Sheffield City Polytechnic (1975-76) and second at the Polytechnic of Wales (1977), where I was a member of the course committee that was led by John Fiske. It was as part of the planning process for this program that we wrote *Reading Television* and came up with the idea of the bardic function.
3. See <en.wikiquote.org/wiki/John_McCarthy>; and see <www-formal.stanford.edu/jmc/>.
4. See <www.santafe.edu/research/topics-dynamics-human-behavior-institutions.php>.

### Acknowledgements

1. UQ Heraldry Project (n.d.) The University of Queensland's Coat of Arms: Historical Aspects', p. 3 (<www.uq.edu.au/about/docs/UQ-coat-of-arms.pdf>).

# References

ADAA [Australian Department of Aboriginal Affairs], Constitutional Section (1981), *Report on a review of the administration of the working definition of Aboriginal and Torres Strait Islander,* AGP, Canberra.

Advanced-television.com (2007, 17 September), 'News Corp boss urges innovation', accessible at <www.advanced-television.com/2007/Sep 17_Sep21.htm>.

*The Age* (2004), 'How a "forbidden" memoir twisted the truth', 24 July, accessible at <www.theage.com.au/articles/2004/07/23/1090464860184. html>.

Allday, D. Helen (1981), *Insurrection in Wales: The Rebellion of the Welsh Led by Owen Glyn Dwr,* Appendix IV, Lavenham, Terence Dalton, Suffolk.

Althusser, Louis (2001), *Lenin and Philosophy and other essays,* NLB, London; Monthly Review Press, New York, accessible at <www.marx2mao. com/Other/LPOE70NB.html>.

Andersen, Robin (2006), A *Century of Media, A Century of War,* Peter Lang, New York.

Annan Report (1977), *Report of the Committee on the Future of Broadcasting,* chaired by Lord [Noel] Annan, HMSO, London.

Arrighi, Giovanni, Iftikhar Ahmad & Min-wen Shih (1996), 'Beyond Western Hegemonies', paper presented at the XXI Meeting of the Social Science History Association, New Orleans, Louisiana, 10—13 October 1996, accessible at <fbc.binghamton.edu/gaht5.htm>.

Arrighi, Giovanni (1994), *The Long Twentieth Century: Money, Power, and the Origins of Our Times,* Verso, London.

*Australian Financial Review* (2004), The secret life of teens', 14 February, p. 20.

Balot, Ryan K. (2001), *Greed and Injustice in Classical Athens,* Princeton University Press, Princeton, NJ.

Barabási, Albert-László (2002), *Linked: The New Science of Networks,* Perseus Publishing, Cambridge, MA.

Barabási, Albert-Laszlo & Eric Bonabeau (2003), 'Scale-free networks', *Scientific American,* May, pp. 50-9, accessible at <www.nd.edu/~networks/

Publication%20Categories/01%20Review%20Articles/ScaleFree_Sci-entific%20Anieri%20288,%2060-69%20(2003).pdf>.

Baran, Paul (1964), *On Distributed Communications: I. Introduction to Distributed Communications Networks,* Rand Corporation, Santa Monica, accessible at<www.rand.org/pubs/research_memoranda/2006/RM3420.pdf>.

Baulch, Emma (2007), *Making Scenes: Reggae, Punk, and Death Metal in 1990s Bali,* Duke University Press, Durham, NC.

Beaton, Cecil (1991), *Chinese Diary and Album,* Oxford University Press, Hong Kong.

Beinhocker, Eric (2006), *The Origin of Wealth: Evolution, Complexity and the Radical Remaking of Economics,* Random House, New York.

Bentley, Alex & Stephen Shennan (2005), 'Random copying and cultural evolution', *Science,* vol. 309, 5 August, pp. 877-9.

Bentley, Tom (1998), *Learning Beyond the Classroom: Educating for a Changing World,* Routledge, London.

Birchall, Clare (2006), 'Cultural studies and the secret', in Gary Hall & Clare Birchall, *New Cultural Studies: Adventures in Theory,* Edinburgh University Press, Edinburgh, pp. 293-311.

Booker, Christopher (2004), *The Seven Basic Plots: Why We Tell Stories,* Continuum, London.

Brecht, Bertholt (1979/80), 'Radio as a means of communication: A talk on the function of radio', *Screen,* 20:3/4, pp. 24-8.

Breward, Chris (2000), 'Cultures, identities, histories: Fashioning a cultural approach to dress', in Nicola White and Ian Griffiths (eds), *The Fashion Business: Theory, Practice, Image,* Berg, Oxford, pp. 23-36.

Brewer, Benjamin (2004), 'The long twentieth century and the cultural turn: World-historical origins of the cultural economy', paper presented at the annual meeting of the American Sociological Association, San Francisco, CA, 14 August, accessible at <www.allacademic.com/meta/p109893_mdex.html>.

Brims, Axel (2005), *Gatewatching: Collaborative Online News Production,* Peter Lang, New York.

Burgess, Jean & Joshua Green (2008), *YouTube: Online Video and Partici-patory Culture,* Polity Press, Cambridge.

Burgess, Jean & John Hartley (2004), 'Digital storytelling: New literacy, new audiences', paper presented at MiT4: The Work of Stories (Fourth Media in Transition conference), MIT, Cambridge (6-8 May), <web.mit.edu/comm-forum/mit4/subs/mit4_abstracts.html>.

Caldwell, John T. (2006), 'Critical industrial practice: Branding, repurposing, and the migratory patterns of industrial texts', *Television & New Media*, 7:2, pp. 99-134.

Campbell, Joseph (1949), *The Hero with a Thousand Faces*, Princeton University Press, Princeton NJ.

Carey, John (1992), *The Intellectuals and the Masses*, Faber & Faber, London.

Carpentier, Nico (2003), 'The BBC's *Video Nation* as a participatory media practice: Signifying everyday life, cultural diversity and participation in an online community', *International Journal of Cultural Studies*, 6:4, pp. 425-47.

Carter, Michael (2003), *Fashion Classics from Carlyle to Barthes*, Berg, Oxford.

CCPR [Centre for Cultural Policy Research] (2003), *Baseline Study on Hong Kong's Creative Industries*, University of Hong Kong for Central Policy Unit HKSAR, Hong Kong, accessible at <ccpr.hku. hk/recent_projects.htm>.

Cheung, Angelica (2005, November), 'Visions of China', *Vogue* UK, no. 2488, vol. 171, pp. 113-18.

Coleman, Stephen (2005), 'New mediation and direct representation: Reconceptualising representation in the digital age', *New Media & Society*, 7(2), pp. 177-98.

College of Arms (n.d.), 'The History of the Royal Heralds and the College of Arms', accessible at <www.college-of-arms.gov.uk/About/01. htm>.

Collier, Paul & Anke Hoeffler (2002), 'The political economy of secession', World Bank/Centre for the Study of African Economies, University of Oxford, and International Peace Research Institute, Oslo, accessible at <users.ox.ac.uk/~ball0144/self-det.pdf>.

Connell, Iain (1984), 'Fabulous powers: Blaming the media', in Len Masternan (ed.), *Television Mythologies: Stars, Shows, Signs*, Routledge/Comedia, London, pp. 88-93.

Cultural Studies Now (2007), *Cultural Studies Now: An international conference*, University of East London. Videos of the keynote speakers can be viewed at <www.uel.ac.uk/culturalstudiesnow/>.

Cunningham, Stuart, John Banks & Jason Potts (2008), 'Cultural economy: The shape of the field', in Helmut K. Anheier & Yudhishthir Raj Isar (eds), *The Cultural Economy* (Cultures and Globalization Series), Sage Publications, Newbury Park, pp. 15-26.

Danwei (2007), 'Is the fake news story fake news?', Danwei.org [Jeff Goldkorn], 20 July, accessible at <www.danwei.org/media_regulation/fake_news_about_fake_news_abou.php>.

Danwei.org (2005, 11 August), 'Vogue China launches' (Jeremy Goldkorn), accessible at <www.danwei.org/media_and_advertising/vogue_china_launches.php>.

Dash, Anil (1999), 'Last refuge of the parentheticals?', Anil Dash blog, 15 August, accessible at <www.dashes.com/anil/1999/08/last-refuge-of. html>.

Derrida, Jacques (1976), *On Grammatology*, Johns Hopkins University Press, Baltimore.

Dodson, Mick (1994), 'The Wentworth Lecture: The end in the beginning: Re(de)fining Aboriginality', *Australian Aboriginal Studies*, vol. 1.

Dopfer, Kurt & Jason Potts (2007), *The General Theory of Economic Evolution* (3rd rev. edn), Routledge, London.

Dutton, Denis (2005), 'Upon a time', *Washington Post*, Sunday, 8 May, BW08, accessible at <www.washingtonpost.com/wp-dyn/content/article/2005/05/05/AR2005050501385_pf.html>.

Dutton, Michael (1998), *Streetlife China*, Cambridge University Press, Cambridge.

Eco, Umberto (1986), *Travels in Hyperreality*, Harcourt Brace Jovanovich, San Diego & New York.

Enzensberger, Hans Magnus (1997), *Critical Essays*, Continuum Books, London & New York.

Enzensberger, Hans Magnus (1974), *The Consciousness Industry: On Literature, Politics, and the Media*, Seabury Press, New York.

Ericson, Richard, Paul Baranek & Janice Chan (1987), *Visualizing Deviance: A Study of News Organizations*, Open University Press, Milton Keynes.

Esty, Jed (2004), *A Shrinking Island: Modernism and National Culture in England*, Princeton University Press, Princeton.

Felski, Rita (1989), *Beyond Feminist Aesthetics*, Harvard University Press, Cambridge.

Fishman, Ted (2004, 4 July), 'The Chinese century', *New York Times Magazine*, accessible at<www.nytimes.com/2004/07/04/magazine/04CHINA. html?ex=1246680000&en=127e32464ca6faB&ei=5088&partner=rss nyt>.

Fiske, John & John Hartley (2003 [1978]), *Reading Television* (new edition), Routledge, London.

Florida, Richard (2002), *The Rise of the Creative Class: and How It's Transforming Work, Leisure, Community and Everyday Life* (with an introduction by Terry Cutler), Pluto Press, Melbourne.

Ford, Patrick K. (1992), *Ystoria Taliesin,* University of Wales Press, Cardiff.

Frow, John (1995), *Cultural Studies and Cultural Value,* Clarendon Press, Oxford.

Gans, Herbert (2004), 'Journalism, journalism education, and democracy', *Journalism & Mass Communication Educator,* 59(1), pp. 10-17.

Garnham, Nicholas (1990), *Capitalism and Communication: Global Culture and the Economics of Information,* Sage Publications, London.

Garnham, Nicholas (1987), 'Concepts of culture: Public policy and the culture industries', *Cultural Studies,* 1:1, pp. 23-38.

Gauntlett, David (1998), 'Ten things wrong with the "effects model"', in R. Dickinson, R. Harindranath & O. Linne (eds), *Approaches to Audiences — A Reader,* Arnold, London, accessible at <www.theory.org.uk/david/ effects.htm>.

Gauntlett, David (2005), *Moving Experiences: Media Effects and Beyond* (2nd edn), John Libbey, London.

Gibson, Mark (2007), *Culture and Power: A History of Cultural Studies,* Berg, Oxford; UNSW Press, Sydney.

Gibson, Mark (2002), 'The powers of the Pokemon: Histories of television, histories of the concept of power', *Media International Australia,* 104, pp. 107-15.

Gitlin, Todd (1993), *The Sixties: Years of Hope, Days of Rage* (rev. edn), Bantam, New York.

Given, J.L. (1907), *Making a Newspaper,* Henry Holt & Co., New York.

Goody, Jack & Ian Watt (1963), 'The consequences of literacy', *Comparative Studies in Society and History,* 5:3, pp. 304-45.

Goulden, Holly & John Hartley (1982), '"Nor should such topics as homosexuality, masturbation, frigidity, premature ejaculation or the menopause be regarded as unmentionable". English literature, school examinations and official discourses', *LTP Journal: Journal of Literature Teaching Politics,* 1, April, pp. 4-20.

Green, K. & J. Sykes (2004), 'Australia needs journalism education accreditation', *JourNet international conference on Professional Education for the Media,* viewed 2 June 2006 at <portal.unesco.org/ci/en/ev.php-URL_ID=19074&URL JDO=DO JTOPIC&URL_SECTION=201. html>.

Griffith, Llewelyn Wyn (1950), *The Welsh,* Pelican Books, Harmondsworth.

Guest, Lady Charlotte (1849), *The Mabinogion,* translated by Lady Charlotte Guest, accessible at <www.gutenberg.org/dirs/etext04/mbnglOh.htm> and at <ebooks.adelaide.edu.au/rn/mabinogion/guest/chapter12.html>.

Hall, Stuart (1981), 'Notes on deconstructing the popular', in R. Samuel (ed), *People's History and Socialist Theory,* Routledge & Kegan Paul, London.

Hall, Stuart (1980), 'Cultural studies: Two paradigms', *Media, Culture and Society, 2,* pp. 57-72.

Hall, Stuart (1973), 'Encoding and decoding in the media discourse', *Stencilled Paper,* no. 7, Birmingham, CCCS.

Hall, Stuart, Iain Connell & Lydia Curti (1977), 'The "unity" of current affairs television', *Working Papers in Cultural Studies, 9.*

Hall, Stuart, Chas Critcher, Tony Jefferson, John Clarke & Brian Robert (1978), *Policing the Crisis: Mugging, the State and Law & Order,* Hutchinson, London.

Halloran, James, Graham Murdock & Philip Elliott (1970), *Demonstrations and Communication: A Case Study,* Penguin Special, Harmondsworth.

Hansen, Søren & Jesper Jensen (1971), *The Little Red Schoolbook,* Stage 1 Publications, London.

Harbage, Alfred (1947), *As They Liked It: An Essay on Shakespeare and Morality,* Macmillan, New York.

Hargreaves, David (2003), *Working Laterally: How Innovation Networks Make an Education Epidemic. Teachers Transforming Teaching,* Demos, London, <www.demos.co.uk/workinglaterally>.

Hargreaves, Ian (1999), 'The ethical boundaries of reporting', in M. Ungersma (ed.), *Reporters and the Reported: The 1999 Vauxhall Lectures on Contemporary Issues in British Journalism,* Centre for Journalism Studies, Cardiff, pp. 1-15.

Hartley, John (2008a), *Television Truths: Forms of Knowledge in Popular Culture,* Blackwell, Oxford.

Hartley, John (2008b), 'The "supremacy of ignorance over instruction and of numbers over knowledge". Journalism, popular culture, and the English constitution', *Journalism Studies,* 9:5, August, pp. 679-91.

Hartley, John (2006), 'The best propaganda: Humphrey Jennings's *The Silent Village* (1943)', in Alan McKee (ed.), *Beautiful Things in Popular Culture,* Blackwell, Oxford, pp. 144-63.

Hartley, John (ed.) (2005), *Creative Industries,* Blackwell, Oxford.

Hartley, John (2004a), 'The "value chain of meaning" and the new economy', *International Journal of Cultural Studies,* 7(1), pp. 129-41.

Hartley, John (2004b), '"Republic of letters" to "television republic"? Citizen readers in the era of broadcast television', in L. Spigel & J. Olsson (eds), *Television after TV: Essays on a Medium in Transition,* Duke University Press, Durham, NC & London, pp. 386-417.

Hartley, John (2003), *A Short History of Cultural Studies,* Sage Publications, London.

Hartley, John (2000), 'Communicational democracy in a redactional society: The future of journalism studies', *Journalism: Theory, Practice, Criticism,* 1(1), pp. 39-47.

Hartley, John (1999), *Uses of Television,* Routledge, London.

Hartley, John (1996), *Popular Reality: Journalism, Modernity, Popular Culture,* Arnold, London.

Hartley, John (1982), *Understanding News,* Routledge, London.

Hartley, John & Kelly McWilliam (eds) (2009), *Story Circle: Digital Storytelling Around the World,* Blackwell, Oxford.

Hartley, John, Greg Hearn, Jo Tacchi & Marcus Foth (2003), 'The Youth Internet Radio Network: A research project to connect youth across Queensland through music, creativity and ICT', in S. Marshall & W. Taylor (eds), *Proceedings of the 5th International Information Technology in Regional Areas (ITiRA) Conference 2003,* Central Queensland University Press, Rockhampton, pp. 335-42.

Hawkes, Terence (1977), *Structuralism and Semiotics,* Methuen, London.

Herman, Edward S. & Noam Chomsky (1988), *Manufacturing Consent: The Political Economy of the Mass Media,* Random House, New York.

Higgs, Peter, Stuart Cunningham & Hasan Bakhshi (2008), *Beyond the Creative Industries: Mapping the Creative Economy in the United Kingdom,* NESTA, London, accessible at <www.nesta.org.uk/assets/Uploads/pdf/Research-Report/beyond__creative_industries_report_NESTA.pdf>.

Hilton, Paris (2004), *Confessions of an Heiress: A Tongue-in-chic Peek behind the Pose,* Simon & Schuster/Fireside, New York.

Hoggart, Paul (2006), 'What my dad did for Lady Chatterley', *The Times,* 18 March, accessible at <entertainment.timesonline.co.uk/tol/arts_and_entertainment/tv_and_radio/article740924.ece>.

Hoggart, Richard (1997), *The Tyranny of Relativism: Culture and Politics in Contemporary English Society,* Transaction Publishers, New Brunswick [published in the UK as *The Way We Live* Now].

Hoggart, Richard (1992), *An Imagined Life,* Chatto & Windus, London.

Hoggart, Richard (1960), 'The uses of television', *Encounter,* vol. XIV, no. 1, pp. 38-45.

Hoggart, Richard (1957), *The Uses of Literacy,* Chatto & Windus, London (1st pb edn, Pelican, Harmondsworth, 1958).

Hoggart, Simon (2006), 'Simon Hoggart's week', *Guardian,* 14 January, accessible at <www.guardian.co.uk/politics/2006/jan/14/politicalcolumnists.politicsx

Hooper, Beverley (1994a), 'From Mao to Madonna: Sources on contemporary Chinese culture', *Southeast Asian Journal of Social Science, 22,* pp. 161-9.

Hooper, Beverley (1994b), 'Women, consumerism and the state in post-Mao China', Asian *Studies Review, 3,* pp. 73-83.

Howkins, John (2002), 'Comments to the Mayor's Commission on the Creative Industries', London, in John Hartley (ed.) (2005), *Creative Industries,* Blackwell, Maiden, MA & Oxford, pp. 117-25.

Hutton, Will [& the Work Foundation] (June 2007), *Staying Ahead: The Economic Performance of the UK Creative Industries,* DCMS, London, accessible at <www.culture.gov.uk/Reference_library/Publications/archive_2007/stayingahead_epukci.htm>.

*The Independent* (2006), 'Bush "planted fake news stories on American TV"', 29 May, accessible at <www.independent.co.uk/news/world/americas/bush-planted-fake-nevvs-stories-on-american-tv-480172. html>.

Jakobson, Roman (1958), 'Closing statement: Linguistics and poetics', in Thomas A. Sebeok (ed.) (1960), *Style and Language,* MIT Press, Cambridge MA, pp. 350-77.

Jenkins, Henry (2006), *Convergence Culture,* NYU Press, New York.

Jenkins, Henry (2004), 'The cultural logic of media convergence', *International Journal of Cultural Studies,* 7(1), pp. 33-44.

Jenkins, Henry (2003), 'Games, the new lively art', in J. Goldstein & J. Raessens (eds), *Handbook of Computer Game Studies,* MIT Press, Cambridge MA.

Jennings, Humphrey (1985), *Pandaemonium: The Coming of the Machine as Seen by Contemporary Observers,* Andre Deutsch/Picador, London.

Jones, Gwyn (1972), *Kings, Beasts and Heroes,* Oxford University Press, Oxford.

Keen, Andrew (2007), *The Cult of the Amateur: How the Democratization of the Digital World Is Assaulting Our Economy, Our Culture, and Our Values,* Doubleday Currency, New York.

Lambert, Joe (2006), *Digital Storytelling: Capturing Lives, Creating Community* (2nd edn), Digital Diner Press, Berkeley, CA.

Lanham, Richard A. (2006), *The Economy of Attention: Style and Substance in the Age of Information*, Chicago University Press, Chicago.

Lawrence, D.H. (1960), *Lady Chatterley's Lover*, Penguin, Harmondsworth.

Leadbeater, Charles (2006), *We-think: The Power of Mass Creativity*, accessible at <www.wethinkthebook.net/book/home.aspx>.

Leadbeater, Charles (2002), *Up the Down Escalator: Why the Global Pessimists Are Wrong*, Viking, London.

Leadbeater, Charles (1999), *Living on Thin Air: The New Economy*, Viking, London.

Leadbeater, Charles & Paul Miller (2004), *The 'Pro-Am' Revolution*, Demos, London, accessed 2 June 2006 from demos.co.uk/catalogue/proameconomy/.

Lee, Richard E. (2004), 'Cultural studies, complexity studies and the transformation of the structures of knowledge', *International Journal of Cultural Studies*, 10(1), pp. 11-20.

Lee, Richard E. (2003), *Life and Times of Cultural Studies: The Politics and Transformation of the Structures of Knowledge*, Duke University Press, Durham, NC.

Lee, Richard E. (1997), 'Cultural studies as *Geisteswissenschaften?* Time, objectivity, and the future of social science', accessible at <fbc.binghamton.edu/rlcs-gws.htm>.

Lees, Jennie Rowley (2008), *The Sydney Eisteddfod Story: 1933-1941*, Currency Press, Sydney.

Leiboff, Marett (2007), *Creative Practice and the Law*, Thomson Lawbooks, Sydney.

Li, Xiaoping (1998) 'Fashioning the body in post-Mao China', in A. Brydon & S. Niessen (eds), *Consuming Fashion: Adorning the Transnational Body*, Berg, Oxford, pp. 71-89.

Lipovetsky, Gilles (1991), *The Empire of Fashion: Dressing Modern Democracy*, Princeton University Press, Princeton.

Lipton, Lenny (1974), *Independent Filmmaking*, Straight Arrow Books, San Francisco; Cassell, London (Studio Vista).

Lotman, Yuri (1990), *The Universe of the Mind; A Semiotic Theory of Culture*, Indiana University Press, Bloomington; I.B.Tauris, London.

Lovink, Geert (ed.) (2008), *My Creativity Reader: A Critique of Creative Industries*, Institute of Network Cultures, Amsterdam.

Lovink, Geert (2003), *Dark Fiber: Tracking Critical Internet Culture,* MIT Press, Cambridge, MA & London.

Lumby, Catharine (1999), *Gotcha! Life in a Tabloid World,* Allen & Unwin, Sydney.

McGuigan, Jim (1992), *Cultural Populism,* Routledge, London.

McWilliam, Erica (2007), 'Unlearning how to teach', paper for Creativity or Conformity? Building Cultures of Creativity in Higher Education, University of Wales Institute, Cardiff, in collaboration with the Higher Education Academy, 8-10 January, accessible at <www.creativityconference.org/presented_papers/McWilliam_Unlearning.doc>.

Matthews, John (2002), *Taliesin: The Last Celtic Shaman,* Inner Traditions/ Bear & Company, Rochester, VT.

MCEETYA [Ministerial Council on Education, Employment, Training & Youth Affairs] (2003), *Australia's Teachers: Australia's Future,* Department of Education Science & Training, Canberra.

Meadows, Daniel (2006), 'New literacies for a participatory culture in the digital age', Community Media Association Festival & AGM <www.comniedia.org.uk/about-cma/cma-events/cma-festival-and-agni-2006/speeches/daniel-meadows-speech/>.

Miller, Toby (ed.) (2001), *A Companion to Cultural Studies,* Blackwell, Oxford.

Miller, Toby (1998), *Technologies of Truth: Cultural Citizenship and the Popular Media,* University of Minnesota Press, Minneapolis.

Morris, Edward D. (1889), The language and literature of Wales', PMLA, vol. 4, no. 1, pp. 4-18, accessible at <http://links.jstor.org/sici?sici=0030-8129%281889%294%3A1%3C4%3ATLALOW%3E2.0.CO%3B2-E>.

Morris, Meaghan (1990), 'Banality in cultural studies', in Patricia Mellencamp (ed.), *Logics of Television: Essays in Cultural Criticism,* Indiana University Press, Bloomington, pp. 14-43.

Nash, D.W. [David William] (1858), *Taliesin; or, The Bards and Druids of Britain. A Translation of the Remains of the Earliest Welsh Bards and an Examination of the Bardic Mysteries,* John Russell Smith, London, accessible at <books.google.com/books?id=SX4NAAAAQAAJ>.

NESTA [National Endowment for Science Technology & the Arts] (April 2006), *Creating Growth: How the UK Can Develop World Class Creative Businesses,* NESTA, London, accessible at <www.nesta.org.uk/assets/pdf/creating_growth_full_report.pdf>.

Newman, Cardinal John (1907), *The Idea of a University: Defined and Illustrated,* Longmans Green, London, accessible at <www.newmanreader.org/works/idea/index.html>.

Oakley, Kate & John Knell (2007), *London's Creative Economy: An Accidental Success?*, The Work Foundation, London.

O'Connor, Justin & Gu Xin (2006), 'A new modernity? The arrival of "creative industries" in China', *International Journal of Cultural Studies*, 9(3).

OECD (2007), *Participative Web and User-Created Content: Web 2.0, Wikis and Social Networking*, OECD, Paris [authored by Sacha Wunsch-Vincent and Graham Vickery], accessible at <www.sourceoecd.org/scienceIT/9789264037465 and www.oecd.org/dataoecd/57/14/38393115.pdf>.

Ormerod, Paul (2001), *Butterfly Economics: A New General Theory of Social and Economic Behavior*, Basic Books, New York.

Owen, Sue (2005), '*The Abuse of Literacy* and the feeling heart: The trials of Richard Hoggart', *Cambridge Quarterly*, 34(2), pp. 147-76.

Popper, Karl (1975), 'The rationality of scientific revolutions', in R. Harré (ed.), *Problems of Scientific Revolutions*, Oxford University Press, Oxford.

Popper, Karl (1972), *Objective Knowledge*, Oxford University Press, Oxford.

Potts, Jason & Stuart Cunningham (2008), 'Four models of the creative industries', *International Journal of Cultural Policy*.

Potts, Jason, Stuart Cunningham, John Hartley & Paul Ormerod (2008), 'Social network markets: A new definition of the creative industries', *Journal of Cultural Economics* (accepted for publication March 2008).

Presser, Helmut (1972), 'Johannes Gutenberg', in Hendrik Vervliet (ed.), *The Book Through 5000 Years*, Phaidon, London & New York, pp. 348-54.

Rees-Mogg, William (2005), 'This is the Chinese century: America may believe it is still at the heart of events, but the future is being shaped on the margins', *The Times*, 3 January, accessible at <www.timeson-line.co.uk/tol/comment/columnists/william_rees_mogg/article407883. ece>.

Rettberg, Jill Walker (2008), *Blogging*, Polity Press, Cambridge.

Rifkin, Jeremy (2000), *The Age of Access: How the Shift from Ownership to Access Is Transforming Modern Life*, Penguin, London.

Ritter, Jonathan (2007), 'Terror in an Andean key: Peasant cosmopolitans interpret 9/11', in Jonathan Ritter & Martin Daughtry (eds), *Music in the Post 9/11 World*, Routledge, New York, pp. 177-208.

Robinson, Ken (2001), *Out of Our Minds: Learning To Be Creative*, Capstone, Oxford.

Roodhouse, Simon (2006), *Cultural Quarters: Principles and Practice,* Intellect Books, Bristol.

Schiller, Herbert (1989), *Culture, Inc.: The Corporate Takeover of Public Expression,* Oxford University Press, New York.

Scientificblogging (2008), 'Stephen Colbert's "truthiness" scientifically validated', Scientificblogging.com News, 24 January, accessible at <www. Scientificblogging.com/news_releases/stephen_col-berts_truthiness_ scientifically_validated>.

Shannon, Claude E. (1948), 'A mathematical theory of communication', reprinted from *The Bell System Technical Journal,* vol. 27, pp. 379-423, 623-56, July, October, accessible at <cm.bell-labs. com/cm/ms/what/ shannonday /shannon1948.pdf>.

Shaw, George Bernard (1937), *The Intelligent Woman's Guide to Socialism, Capitalism, Sovietism and Fascism* (2 vols), Pelican Books, Harmondsworth (first published 1928).

Shenkar, Oded (2004), *The Chinese Century: The Rising Chinese Economy and Its Impact on the Global Economy, the Balance of Power, and Your Job,* Wharton School Publishing, Philadelphia.

Shirky, Clay (2008), *Here Comes Everybody: The Power of Organizing Without Organizations,* Penguin, New York.

Shuttleworth, Alan (1966), *Two Working Papers in Cultural Studies - A Humane Centre* and *Max Weber and the 'Cultural Sciences'* (Occasional Paper no. 2), Centre for Contemporary Cultural Studies, Birmingham University.

Sinfield, Alan (1997), *Literature, Politics and Culture in Postwar Britain* (rev. edn), Continuum, London.

Sokal, Alan D. (2000), *The Sokal Hoax: The Sham that Shook the Academy* (edited by the editors of *Lingua Franca),* University of Nebraska Press, Lincoln.

Sonesson, Goran (2002), 'The culture of Modernism: From transgressions of art to arts of transgression', in M. Carani & G. Sonesson (eds), Visio, 3, 3: *Modernism,* pp. 9-26, accessible at <www.arthist. lu.se/kultsem/ sonesson/Culture%20of%20Mod3.html>.

Sonesson, Goran (1997), 'The limits of nature and culture in cultural semiotics', in Richard Hirsch (ed.), *Papers from the Fourth Bi-annual Meeting of the Swedish Society for Semiotic Studies,* Linkoping University, December, accessible at <www.arthist.lu.se/kultsem/sonesson/ CultSeml.html>.

Steele, Valerie (2000), 'Fashion: Yesterday, today and tomorrow', in W. White & I. Griffiths (eds), *The Fashion Business: Theory, Practice, Image,* Berg, Oxford, pp. 7-20.

Stevens and Associates (2003), *The National Eisteddfod of Wales: The Way Forward,* Eisteddfod Genedlaethol Cymru, Cardiff, accessible at <www. bwrdd-yr-iaith.org.uk/download.php/pID=44756>.

Tacchi, Jo, Greg Hearn & Abe Ninan (2004), 'Ethnographic action research: A method for implementing and evaluating new media technologies', in K. Prasad (ed.), *Information and Communication Technology: Recasting Development,* BR Publishing Corporation, Delhi.

Terranova, Tiziana (2000), 'Free labor: Producing culture for the digital economy', *Social Text,* 63, vol. 18, no. 2, Summer, pp. 33—57, accessible at <www.btinternet.com/~t.terranova/freelab.html>.

Terranova, Tiziana (2004), *Network Culture: Politics for the Information Age,* Pluto, London.

Throsby, D. (2001), *Economics and Culture,* Cambridge University Press, Cambridge.

Turner, Graeme (2005), *Ending the Affair: The Decline of Current Affairs in Australia,* UNSW Press, Sydney.

Turner, Graeme (2002), *British Cultural Studies* (3rd edn), Routledge, London.

UN (1948) *Universal Declaration of Human Rights,* adopted by the General Assembly of the UN, 10 December, viewed 2 June 2006at<unhchr.ch/ udhr/miscinfo/carta.htm>.

UNFPA (2007a), *State of World Population 2007,* accessible at <www. unfpa.org/swp/2007/english/introduction.html>.

UNFPA (2007b), *Growing Up Urban: State of World Population 2007, Youth Supplement,* p. v, accessible at <www.unfpa.org/upload/lib_pub_ file/702_filename_youth_swop_eng.pdf>.

Veblen, Thorstein (1899), *The Theory of the Leisure Class,* Bantam, New York, accessible at <xroads.Virginia.edu/~hyper/VEBLEN/veblenhp. html>.

Veblen, Thorstein (1964), 'The economic theory of women's dress', in Leon Ardzrooni (ed.), *Essays in Our Changing Order: The Writings of Thorstein Veblen,* Augustus M. Kelly, New York.

Vonnegut, Kurt (1981), *Palm Sunday: An Autobiographical Collage,* Jonathan Cape, London.

Warner, Michael (2002), *Publics and Counterpublics,* Zone Books, New York.

Whitman, Walt (1883 [1995]), *Specimen Days and Collect,* Dover, New York.

Who, The (1973), 'Helpless dancer', *Quadrophenia* (lyrics accessible at <www.quadrophenia.net/>).

Williams, Raymond (1974), 'Communications as cultural science', *Journal of Communication,* 24 (3), pp. 26-38.

Williams, Raymond (1973), 'Base and superstructure in Marxist cultural theory', *New Left Review,* 1/82, accessible (fee) at <newleftreview. org/?page=article&view= 1568>.

Williams, Raymond (1961), *Culture and Society 1780-1950,* Penguin, Harmondsworth.

Windschuttle, Keith (2000), 'The poverty of cultural studies', *Journalism Studies,* 1(1), pp. 145-59.

Zhao, Feifei (2005, 21 July), 'China's in vogue so *Vogue's* in China', *China View* (www.chinaview.cn), accessible at <news.xinhuanet. com/english/200 5-07/21 /content_3248190,htm>.

Zittrain, Jonathan (2008), *The Future of the Internet - and How to Stop It,* Yale University Press, Cambridge; Penguin Books, London, accessible at <fu tureoftheinternet.org/>.

# Acknowledgements

The most important acknowledgement here is to the work and career of Richard Hoggart. He won't necessarily remember this, but he kick-started my career in the 1970s, when he was Warden of Goldsmiths College, by *not* giving me a job as a lecturer in Shakespearean drama, despite the fact that I was a passionate follower of the most provocative Shakespearean scholar of the time, Terence Hawkes. Hoggart encouraged me instead to press on with this new-fangled work in cultural and media studies, which I did. When it comes to sparking my own ideas off the flint of his, I'm a serial offender. My books *Uses of Television (*1999) and *A Short History of Cultural Studies* (2003) are especially indebted to him. Richard Hoggart has been a great role model, not least for his willingness to engage with public policy and institutional modernisation while retaining an influential stream of critical, journalistic and scholarly output. So I'm proud to pinch his title (once again), and to dedicate to him this effort to pull off the same trick, in the full knowledge that he may take a 'robust' view of some of its arguments and ideas.

Closer to home, and themselves the inspiration for a future-oriented approach, I would like to thank my Federation Fellowship team, past and present:

- Dr John Banks, Dr Jean Burgess, Dr Lucy Montgomery, Dr Kelly McWilliam, Dr Ellie Rennie (postdoctoral fellows)
- Dr Joshua Green, Dr Bao Jiannu, Woitek Konzal, Dr Li Hui, Henry Siling Li, Thomas Petzold, Dr Aneta Podkalicka, Dr Christine Schmidt, Dr Jinna Tay, Shannon Wylie (PhD students), Nicki Hunt,

Rebekah Denning, Claire Carlin, Tina Horton (research project support) and Eli Koger (multimedia research assistance).

The ARC Centre of Excellence for Creative Industries and Innovation (CCI) has provided an invaluable and stimulating collegiate culture, not to mention good company, and I'm grateful to all staff. Special thanks go to director Stuart Cunningham, to the chair of our advisory board, Terry Cutler, and to Centre Fellow Jason Potts, who between them have challenged my thinking, root and branch. What more could one ask of a colleague?

Well, Oliver-style, one can simply ask for more, including further intellectual dialogue. So now Stuart and I are co-editing the book series of which this is a 'launch' volume. *Creative Economy + Innovation Culture* is the first new book series to be offered by the University of Queensland Press (UQP) in more than a decade, and its launch coincides with the centenary year of the *University of Queensland Act* of 1909. It is therefore quite a coup for us, not least given our location at Queensland University of Technology (QUT), the technological university 'down the river' from sandstone University of Queensland (UQ). This collaboration among local rivals speaks volumes - literally - for the revitalising energy of the work that Stuart and I have been pursuing at the CCI, and which our series seeks to foster, namely the dialogue between cultural and economic perspectives on social change and the growth of knowledge. In fact, such collaborative effort among unlikely partners for useful ends brings to the fore the original egalitarian purpose of higher education in Queensland, as promulgated by Premier William Kidston in 1909 when UQ was established:

I would not have it forgotten that Queensland is a hive of working bees, and that all our educational institutions, from Kindergarten to University, should keep that fact in view. There is this difference between the youngest University in the Empire and the oldest: Oxford was established by a King; the University of Queensland is established by the people.[1]

Finally, I must thank the three anonymous reviewers of the manuscript for UQP: generous, critical, informed and helpful, they brought to the process of revising the book the convivial pleasures of the 'working bee', dispelling the solitariness of scholarly labour, even though I fear I may have ignored their most inspired suggestions and resisted their most urgent pleas to avoid the pitfalls of my own ignorance.

John Hartley is the recipient of an Australian Research Council Federation Fellowship. The research was conducted at the Australian Research Council Centre of Excellence for Creative Industries and Innovation, with assistance on some aspects from the ARC Cultural Research Network. The book includes material revised from papers and chapters as follows:

- John Hartley (2008), 'Repurposing literacy: The uses of Richard Hoggart for creative education', in Sue Owen (ed.), *Richard Hoggart and Cultural Studies,* Palgrave, London.
- John Hartley (2009), 'From the consciousness industry to creative industries: Consumer-created content, social network markets and the growth of knowledge', in Jennifer Holt & Alisa Perren (eds), *Media Industries: History, Theory and Methods,* Blackwell, Oxford.
- John Hartley (2009), 'TV stories: From the "bardic function" to the "eisteddfod function"', in John Hartley & Kelly McWilliam (eds), Story *Circle: Digital Storytelling Around the World,* Blackwell, Oxford.
- John Hartley (2008), 'Uses of YouTube: Digital literacy and the growth of knowledge', in Jean Burgess & Joshua Green (2008), *YouTube,* Polity Press, Cambridge.

- John Hartley (2008), 'Problems of expertise and scalability in self-made media', in Knut Lundby (ed.), *Digital Storytelling, Mediatized Stories: Self-representations in New Media,* Peter Lang, New York.
- John Hartley (2008), 'Journalism as a human right: the cultural approach to journalism', in Martin Loffelholz & David Weaver (eds), *Global Journalism Research: Theories, Methods, Findings, Future,* Blackwell, Oxford, pp. 39-51.
- John Hartley & Lucy Montgomery (2009), 'Fashion as consumer entrepreneurship: Emergent risk culture, social network markets and the launch of *Vogue* in China', *Chinese Journal of Communication,* vol. 1, no. 2.
- John Hartley (2008), ' "The future is an open future". Cultural studies at the end of the "long twentieth century" and the beginning of the "Chinese century"', paper presented at 'Creative destruction: Lessons for science and innovation policy from the rise of the creative industries', joint research workshop of CCI (ARC Centre of Excellence for Creative Industries and Innovation) and FEAST (Forum for European-Australian Science and Technology cooperation), State Library of Queensland, Brisbane, 27-28 March.

# Index

communication *(cont.)*
    effective  96
    ethical  161
    mass  14, 46, 47, 151
    one-way  46, 49, 204
    phatic  112, 114
    Shannon's model  46
    theory  121
    two-way 47
communism 7
complexity studies 62, 197, 204, 211, 215
consciousness industry  44
consumer co-creation  13, 202
consumerism  9, 18
consumers  14, 64
    entrepreneurship  12
    increasing power  13
    socially networked  56
    *vs* users  64
consumption  13, 45
convergence culture  186
copyright  14, 45, 218n
Council for National Academic Awards
    212, 225n
creative class  31-2
Creative Commons  66, 129
creative destruction  64-7, 177, 194-8, 205, 211, 214, 217
creative industries  14, 27, 45, 49-58, 62, 204-5, 217
    DCMS' cluster model  54-5, 56, 59
    emerging knowledge  69
    importance  204-8
    NESTA model  56-7, 59
    phases  53,70
    Work Foundation economy
        model  59-60
creativity  13, 25, 31, 46, 50, 101, 215
    demand model  60-1
    fostering  32, 33
    need for  107
    provider model  60
    reflexive  216

critical citizenship  5, 17
critical literacy  2, 4, 20, 23
critics  4, 5, 6, 196
cultural science  212-13, 214-15
cultural studies  8, 38, 39, 111, 143-5, 196, 210
    conjunctural analysis  191
    crisis of representation  198-9
    and emergent institutions  203
    and journalism  142-3, 146-7, 148-9
    philosophy of plenty  185-6
    power model  202-3
    and social change  191-4
    Western enterprise  187,190
    Williamson  213
culture  101, 112, 197, 205, 216
    role in society  144-5
    shaped by media  38
    and social change  194
    Tartu school semiotic model  80
    Williams' schema  51-2
cyber-bullying  22ln
cyber-democracy  14

Dash, Anil  114-15
Davies, Donald  47
daydreaming  26-7, 29, 105, 107
Demarchelier, Patrick  179, 181
democracy  19, 84, 148, 152
demonstrations  10-11, 188
    Grosvenor Square  9-11
digital literacy
    compared with print literacy 104-7
    creative  18, 67-8, 69
    defined  21
    left to the market  104
    production of digital content 12, 103
    and teachers  34
    of teenagers  30
    uses  9, 12, 187, 217
    and YouTube  107-8
digital media
    creative content  106

storytelling *(cont.)*
  early  73, 115
  functions of profession  97-8
  inductive reasoning  119-21
  mass participation  84-5, 95-6
  plots  115-16, 118, 124
  stages of a story  118-19
  use of language  87
  *see also* digital storytelling
struggle  9, 11, 211
systems  15

*Taketori Monogatari*  93
Taliesin  73-6, 81, 86, 92, 97
  brand name  220n
Taliesin function  97
taste-formation  4, 6, 8
Taylor, Adegoke  207
teachers  18, 32
  educating  29-30
  learning entrepreneurs  37
  new objectives  33-4
teamwork  26
teenagers  26-8, 205, 206
  and creative industries  208
  daydreaming  26-7, 29, 105
  innate digital skills  104-5
  secret life  29-30
  self-expression  28
  self-indulgence  70
  shaped by media  28, 38
television  18, 49, 108, 124
  audience  75-6, 83
  bardic function  72, 75-82, 108
Tennant, David  2-4
tension, cultural  28
Terfel, Bryn  91
*The Chatterley Affair*  2
*The Little Red Schoolbook*  188
*The Origin of Wealth*  164-5
*The Silent Village*  133
*The Uses of Literacy*  1, 2, 6, 17, 18, 24, 157
truth, 'other ways of being in'  2, 6, 26

United Nations  205-6
United States  208, 209
Universal Declaration of Human Rights (UN)  148-9, 154, 155, 157
universities  24, 37, 38, 104
  ICT skills  105, 106, 130
University of Queensland  241-2
urban species  205-6
user-created content  39, 42, 49, 55-6, 64, 203
  creative destruction  64-7
  sociocultural impacts  65-6
  value adding  123
  *see also* self-made media content

values  6, 63, 211
Veblen, Thorstein  163-4, 176
*Vogue*  166, 177, 183
Vogue Australia  180
Vogue Britain  181-2
Vogue China  167, 175-80, 181, 182
  launch cover  179
Vogue Paris  180-1
Vonnegut, Kurt  140

*Waiting for Fidel*  135
Wales  127, 128
Wang Wenqin  179
*War of the Worlds*  116
Ward, Gemma  179, 180, 181
Web 2.0  40, 46, 64, 184, 200, 203
Western civilisation  189-90
Whitman, Wilt  71, 99
Wikipedia  69, 105, 129
Wilde, Oscar  4
Williams, Raymond  51, 111, 212, 213
Wilson, Elizabeth  173, 176
Wintour, Anna  182, 184
working class  31, 146, 192
  culture  22, 28, 145
writing  19, 23, 98
writing public  158